CATAN®

THE OFFICIAL

COOKBOOK

CATAN®

COOKBOOK

ULYSSES PRESS

Thank you to Klaus Teuber for creating CATAN—
a game that brings us all together.

Special thanks to Arnd Beenen, Bianca Freund, and Sonja Krützfeldt at CATAN GmbH, to Morgan Dontanville and Kelli Schmitz at CATAN Studio, and to Katha Busk, Danielle Robb, and Alexander Thieme at Asmodee Entertainment.

Published by:
ULYSSES PRESS
PO Box 3440
Berkeley, CA 94703
www.ulyssespress.com

ISBN: 978-1-64604-452-8
Library of Congress Control Number: 2022944084

Printed in China
2 4 6 8 10 9 7 5 3 1

Front cover and interior design: David Hastings
Production: what!design @ whatweb.com
Photographs: Allyson Reedy and Greg McBoat

For Catanians far and wide

Introduction

Welcome, adventurers! If you're holding this book, you are probably no stranger to one of the most popular board games of all time: CATAN®. Internationally beloved, CATAN is the powerful universal story of humankind's quest to explore the world—to discover, trade, build, and settle.

In a CATAN game, you become an adventurous settler carving out a home on an uncharted island. Violence holds no sway in CATAN. Cleverness, flexibility, and adaptability are your keys to victory.

While no two CATAN games can ever be the same, every game requires a community of friends and family to come together, communicate, and collaborate in order for one Catanian to win the day! This spirit is the key to making CATAN infinitely playable and endlessly fun.

For fans looking to expand the spirit of CATAN beyond the game board, nothing builds community like a hearty meal. Now you can bring your fellow Catanians together with food, whether it's to break bread (see Harvest Dinner Rolls, page 128), feast on a hearty rack of lamb (see Great Hall Rack of Lamb, page 107), or toast to victory (see Victory Point Punch, page 175).

The selection of recipes in this book offers something for everyone, including vegetarian variations and meals for cooks of different skill levels. Each recipe has a fun CATAN-themed spin, whether it's a punny reference to your favorite development card (see Ear of Plenty Corn Dip, page 17), a resource-inspired main dish (see Chicken under a Brick, page 91), or simply an easy game-night snack you could imagine coming from the island of Catan (see Tavern Pretzel Bites and Beer Cheese, page 41).

Recipes are organized into four parts. Part I, Game (K)night Snacks, features bites, appetizers, and finger foods easy to make for a crowd. Part II offers Food for the Road, with lighter breakfast and lunch fare that can be enjoyed during the day, whether you're building the longest road or making clever trades at work. Part III, Adventurer's Feast, has heartier entrees and side dishes for a more formal dinner or over-the-top celebration. Part IV, Hard-Won Desserts, includes delicious treats for late-night gaming. Finally, Part V, Cheers for Victory, offers a selection of mostly alcoholic (some nonalcoholic variations are included) cocktails perfect for a cozy night of gaming.

So before you break out your game box, take a spin through the delicious recipes in this book and stock up on crucial provisions! Whether you're planning a game night, an all-day board game marathon, or just an evening of casual fun, now you can enjoy CATAN in a whole new way!

Throughout this cookbook, you will find symbols indicating any dietary restrictions that the recipe adheres to. For the purposes of this book, we define "Sugar-Free" as no added refined sugar. Please refer to the key below as you explore:

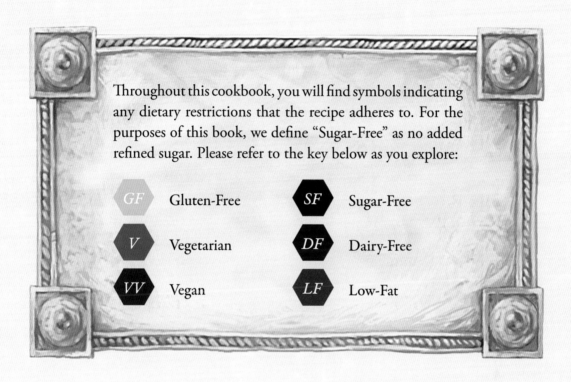

GF — Gluten-Free

V — Vegetarian

VV — Vegan

SF — Sugar-Free

DF — Dairy-Free

LF — Low-Fat

PART I

Game (K)night Snacks

Tasty Appetizers, Delicious Dips, and Hearty Munchies

Explorers on Horseback

Ear of Plenty Corn Dip

SEVEN-Layer Dip

Forager's Veggie Platter

Forest Dweller's Dip

The Longest Road Mix

All-Nighter Energy Bites

Caramelized Pear and Sheep's Milk Cheese Mini-Tarts

Manchego Cheese Crackers

Cottage Cheese Mini Quiches

Scalded Feta Barbarian Skewers

Merchants in a Blanket

Toasts for Traders

Tavern Pretzel Bites and Beer Cheese

Seaworthy Beef Jerky

Stuffed Mushrooms with Fresh Island Herbs

Adventurer's Charcuterie Board

Explorers on Horseback

A hearty snack for any explorer, this variation on the popular "devils on horseback" appetizer is easier on the spice for a crowd-pleasing snack that is extremely easy to make. Double or triple if you're feeding a big group of Catanians.

SERVES
4 to 6

PREP TIME
15 minutes

COOK TIME
10 to 15 minutes

16 Marcona almonds or smoked almonds

2 ounces Manchego cheese, cut into small pieces

16 Medjool dates, pitted

8 slices prosciutto, halved lengthwise, or 16 strips thin-cut bacon

INSTRUCTIONS

1. Preheat the oven to 400°F.

2. Place one almond and one small piece of cheese into the center of each date (in place of the pit). Pinch to reseal.

3. Wrap each date with a piece of prosciutto or bacon and place seam-side down on a rimmed baking sheet.

4. Bake for 10 to 12 minutes for prosciutto, or until the prosciutto is gently browned. Bake for 12 to 15 minutes for bacon, or until it is crisp.

DID YOU KNOW? The first edition of CATAN was published in Germany in 1995.

Ear of Plenty Corn Dip

The Year of Plenty development card can be a game changer, especially when there's a shortage of a specific resource in the market. This recipe not only pays homage to the iconic card but also is a unique dip for your corn chips. Plentifully packed with starchy kernels, fresh herbs, cheese, and flavorful seasonings, this dip makes for the most colorful occasion, served with blue corn tortilla chips.

SERVES
4 to 6

PREP TIME
10 minutes

COOK TIME
10 minutes

3 fresh ears corn, shucked

1 teaspoon smoked paprika

½ cup Mexican crema
(or ½ cup sour cream whisked with 1 tablespoon lime juice)

2 tablespoons crumbled cotija cheese

2 tablespoons minced fresh cilantro

blue corn tortilla chips, for serving

INSTRUCTIONS

1. Preheat a grill to medium-high heat. Grill the corn until it is barely charred on all sides, about 7 to 8 minutes total.

2. Slice the corn kernels from the corncob into a bowl.

3. Whisk in the paprika, crema, cotija, and cilantro.

4. Serve at room temperature with blue corn tortilla chips.

SEVEN-Layer Dip

Seasoned players know if you are sitting on a lot of resources, a seven can strip you of a brilliant game plan. Luckily, this hearty, no-fuss seven-layer bean dip won't leave you feeling robbed! It combines easy prep items with cheese, spices, and fresh ingredients to create the perfect snack moment. Be sure to make ahead so it's chilled in time for your game night—probability is also high this will be scooped up before the last victory point is won.

SERVES
4 to 6

PREP TIME
10 minutes, plus
2 hours to chill

1 (16-ounce) can seasoned refried beans

1 cup prepared guacamole

1½ cups sour cream

2 teaspoons smoked paprika

1 tablespoon lime juice

2 cups shredded cheddar cheese

4 roma tomatoes, diced

2 scallions, thinly sliced

8 black olives, thinly sliced

corn tortilla chips, for serving

INSTRUCTIONS

1. Spread the refried beans in a shallow dish.

2. Spread the guacamole over the refried beans.

3. In a separate container, whisk the sour cream, smoked paprika, and lime juice. Spread this over the beans. Top with the cheese, then tomatoes, scallions, and olives. Chill for at least 2 hours in the fridge.

4. Serve chilled with tortilla chips.

Forager's Veggie Platter

A snack table isn't complete without at least one healthy snack—Catanians can't survive on jerky and chips alone! Including blanched veggies helps elevate this crudité from your standard premade veggie plate. Make sure to forage your produce aisles for the freshest vegetables, and feel free to add any other vegetables that may be in season. This pairs well with any of your favorite dips, but we prefer the freshness of the Forest Dweller's Dip (page 21).

SERVES
4 to 6

PREP TIME
15 minutes

COOK TIME
5 to 7 minutes

8 ounces green beans, trimmed

2 bunches broccolini

1 bunch radishes, trimmed

8 carrots, peeled and cut into spears

1 pint grape tomatoes

2 yellow, orange, or red bell peppers, cored and cut into spears

INSTRUCTIONS

1. Bring a large pot of salted water to a boil.

2. Fill a large bowl with cold water and add several cups of ice cubes.

3. Cook the green beans in the boiling water for 3 to 4 minutes, until bright green. Use tongs to remove the green beans and immediately place them into the ice water. Transfer to a colander to drain as soon as they're cool, about 2 minutes. Add more ice to the water in the bowl to bring the temperature back down.

4. Add the broccolini to the pot and cook for 2 to 3 minutes, until bright green. Use tongs to remove the broccolini and immediately place them into the ice water. Transfer to a colander to drain as soon as they're cool, about 2 minutes.

5. Pat the broccolini and green beans dry with paper towels.

6. Arrange the vegetables on a serving platter, alternating colors as you wish.

7. Serve with the Forest Dweller's Dip that follows, or your favorite creamy salad dressing.

Forest Dweller's Dip

It's easy to imagine the fresh, herbaceous smell of Catan's forests while scooping up some of this creamy vegetable-friendly dip. Using fresh herbs is this dip's strength and what raises it above a premade dressing. Serve with Forager's Veggie Platter (page 20).

MAKES
2 cups

PREP TIME
10 minutes

1 cup sour cream

1 cup mayonnaise

¼ cup minced fresh chives

2 tablespoons minced fresh parsley

1 tablespoon minced fresh tarragon

1 teaspoon balsamic vinegar

sea salt, to taste

freshly ground pepper, to taste

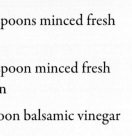

INSTRUCTIONS

1. Place all of the ingredients into a blender and blend until combined. Season to taste with salt and pepper.

The Longest Road Mix

Go for that Longest Road with the salty-sweet energy boost from this trail mix packed with nuts, dried fruits, and sweets. Easily prep ahead or on game night with (mostly) healthy, simple ingredients you can find anywhere, and enjoy whether you're vegetarian or gluten-free.

MAKES
8 cups

PREP TIME
5 minutes

2 cups roasted unsalted peanuts

2 cups roasted salted almonds

2 cups dried banana chips

1 cup chocolate chips

1 cup dried cranberries

INSTRUCTIONS

1. Combine all of the ingredients in a large bowl. Store in an airtight container.

DID YOU KNOW? The United States is the only place where the robber appears as a single figure. In Germany and the rest of the world, the robber appears as three suspicious-looking felllows.

All-Nighter Energy Bites

This anytime appetizer is jam-packed with nuts and chocolate for a healthy, sweet, and protein-loaded snack. The no-bake recipe makes it easy for beginner and intermediate chefs alike to save their energy for an all-night CATAN-athon. Whip up these energy bites a day or a week in advance and store them in the fridge for best results. They're easy to make and don't require any special equipment like candy thermometers or molds. They also make for a great pre-workout snack, family-friendly treat, and welcome addition to a finger-food smorgasbord for a full-fledged game night.

SERVES
8

PREP TIME
5 minutes

COOK TIME
5 minutes

1 cup almond butter or peanut butter

½ cup maple syrup

½ teaspoon vanilla extract

1 cup dark chocolate chips

1 cup almonds, roughly chopped

1 cup pecans, roughly chopped

2 cups Rice Krispies

½ teaspoon flaky sea salt

INSTRUCTIONS

1. Heat the almond butter, maple syrup, and vanilla in a small saucepan over low heat until bubbling.

2. In a large heatproof bowl, mix the chocolate chips, almonds, pecans, and Rice Krispies. Pour in the almond butter mixture and stir with a spatula. The heat from the almond butter mixture will melt the chocolate chips somewhat.

3. Line an 8 x 8-inch baking dish with parchment paper or plastic wrap. Spread the mixture out into the pan and pat down gently with the spatula. Sprinkle with the sea salt.

4. Refrigerate until ready to serve. Cut into 2 x 2-inch bites.

Caramelized Pear and Sheep's Milk Cheese Mini-Tarts

SERVES
4 to 6

PREP TIME
10 minutes

COOK TIME
10 minutes

Evoke the many pastures of Catan with these elevated game night hors d'oeuvres made with Roquefort, a blue cheese made from sheep's milk. The unique ingredients make the recipe memorable as well as delicious, and the savory and sweet treats work as either a mini meal or a snack. Combine with Wheat Berry Salad (page 79) or Fall Harvest Salad (page 81) for a complete meal.

2 tablespoons butter, divided

2 pears, ripe but still somewhat firm, peeled and diced

2 tablespoons brown sugar, divided

4 ounces Roquefort cheese, crumbled

¼ cup finely chopped walnuts

1 (2-ounce) box mini phyllo tart shells

INSTRUCTIONS

1. Heat 1 tablespoon of the butter in a large skillet over medium-high heat until it is melted and begins to foam.

2. In a separate bowl, toss the pears with 1 tablespoon of the brown sugar and then transfer to the skillet. Cook for 4 to 5 minutes, until the pears break down and begin to brown.

3. Return the pears to the mixing bowl and add the Roquefort. Stir gently to mix.

4. In the same skillet, melt the remaining butter then add the remaining 1 tablespoon of brown sugar and the walnuts. Cook for 2 minutes over medium-high heat until the mixture smells toasty, about 2 minutes.

5. Place the phyllo tart shells on a serving platter. Divide the pear and cheese mixture between them. Top with the walnut and butter mixture. Serve warm or at room temperature.

Manchego Cheese Crackers

SERVES
4 to 6

PREP TIME
10 minutes, plus
1 hour to chill

COOK TIME
15 to 18 minutes

There are many varieties of sheep's cheese out there, but Manchego is at the top of the list for easy access and decadent flavor. These crackers use that cheese to make one of the tastiest homemade snacks around. Tip: allow the dough to chill fully before baking, but don't leave it in the fridge too long or it'll be hard to roll out in time to place your starting settlement. Let cool completely and serve as a stand-alone snack or combined with your favorite cheese and veggie toppings, like SEVEN-Layer Dip (page 18) or fresh mango salsa.

6 ounces Manchego cheese, shredded

1 cup all-purpose flour

½ tablespoon cornstarch

¼ teaspoon fine sea salt

1 tablespoon minced fresh rosemary

⅓ cup cold butter, cut into small pieces

2 tablespoons ice water

½ teaspoon flaky sea salt

INSTRUCTIONS

1. Place the shredded cheese, flour, cornstarch, fine salt, rosemary, and butter into a food processor. Pulse a few times until the mixture resembles coarse sand. Add the ice water and pulse until the dough comes together.

2. Wrap the dough tightly in plastic wrap and refrigerate for 1 hour.

3. Preheat the oven to 350°F.

4. Cut a sheet of parchment paper that's roughly the size of your baking sheet. On the parchment paper, roll the dough out to about 10 x 14 inches. Cut it into 2 x 5-inch rectangles. Season with the flaky sea salt.

5. Carefully slide the parchment paper onto the baking sheet and separate the rectangles gently. Bake for 15 to 18 minutes, or until they're gently browned on the edges. Slide the crackers onto a cooling rack and allow to cool completely before serving.

Cottage Cheese Mini Quiches

SERVES
4 to 6

PREP TIME
10 minutes

COOK TIME
15 to 18 minutes

While sheep's milk cottage cheese would be on theme, any type of cottage cheese you can get your hands on works for this low-energy, high-reward hors d'oeuvre. Increase the amount of bell peppers if you want to make a meat-free version of this dish, and serve the quiches up hot or cold—they're amazing either way. This is the perfect prep-ahead treat for whatever gathering you have in mind.

15 mini phyllo pastry shells

8 ounces cottage cheese

3 eggs

¼ teaspoon sea salt

½ teaspoon freshly ground black pepper

1 teaspoon minced fresh rosemary

4 ounces shredded Italian cheese blend

½ cup finely diced bell pepper

½ cup cooked sausage

SF

INSTRUCTIONS

1. Preheat the oven to 400°F. Place the phyllo shells into a mini muffin tin.

2. Combine the cottage cheese, eggs, salt, pepper, rosemary, and shredded cheese in a medium mixing bowl. Stir in the bell pepper and sausage. Use a small measuring cup to evenly divide the quiche mixture into the phyllo shells. Bake for 15 to 18 minutes, or until the quiches are set.

Scalded Feta Barbarian Skewers

This super-quick recipe is not only easy to make but doubles as a fun activity for the whole party. Prep the ingredients with high-quality feta to ensure the cheese holds up, and chill thoroughly so it won't crumble when it comes time to skewer the ingredients. Serve up as a snack, main, or side dish, depending on your mood.

SERVES
6

PREP TIME
10 minutes

COOK TIME
10 to 12 minutes

1 (8-ounce) block sheep's milk feta, cut into 12 cubes

12 dates, pitted

1 French baguette, torn into 12 cubes

12 strips bacon, halved

extra-virgin olive oil, for drizzling

sea salt, to taste

freshly ground pepper, to taste

SF

INSTRUCTIONS

1. Thread 1 piece of feta onto a skewer, followed by 1 date and 1 cube of bread. Repeat so that there are two of each ingredient on each skewer.

2. Wrap the bacon around each slice of feta. Repeat with the remaining skewers.

3. Drizzle the skewers with olive oil and season with salt and pepper. Place on a preheated gas or charcoal grill and cook for about 10 to 12 minutes, turning frequently to gently brown the bacon.

Merchants in a Blanket

For a twist on a classic party snack, try these pigs in a blanket. They're a bit spicier than average, using Cajun-style andouille sausage, but still easy and utterly delicious. Make fresh for the best results, but if you know you're going to be slammed night-of, whip them up ahead of time, refrigerate, and pop them in the oven when it's time.

SERVES
4

PREP TIME
10 minutes

COOK TIME
25 minutes

2 sheets frozen puff pastry

1 pound cooked Cajun-style andouille sausage

1 egg

1 tablespoon milk

SF

INSTRUCTIONS

1. Preheat the oven to 400°F. Line a rimmed baking sheet with parchment paper.

2. Slice each of the puff pastry sheets in half widthwise, so that you have 2 shorter rectangles. Place a sausage into the center of each puff pastry sheet and roll it up, placing it seam-side down on the baking sheet. Repeat with the remaining sausages and pastry sheets.

3. Whisk the egg and milk together in a small bowl. Use a pastry brush to brush the egg wash over each of the pastry bundles.

4. Bake for 25 minutes, or until the pastry is golden brown and the sausages are heated through.

Toasts for Traders

Perfect for game night, holidays, or any other time you just want some carb-y goodness, these three flavored toasts are the perfect choice for an easy, quick snack. Use that French baguette to make one or all three flavors for a single gathering. They pair perfectly with the Green Garden Smoothie (page 61) or a Mug of Barley Soup (page 67) for a full meal you and yours will love.

SERVES
4 to 6

PREP TIME
10 minutes

COOK TIME
5 minutes

1 French baguette, sliced in ¾-inch pieces

TRADITIONAL BRUSCHETTA

1 pint grape tomatoes, halved

¼ cup minced fresh basil

3 tablespoons extra-virgin olive oil, divided

2 teaspoons good-quality balsamic vinegar

pinch of sea salt

TRADITIONAL BRUSCHETTA

1. Combine the tomatoes, basil, 1 tablespoon of the olive oil, and balsamic vinegar. Add a generous pinch of sea salt. Set aside.

2. Heat the remaining 2 tablespoons of olive oil in a large cast-iron skillet. Toast a third of the bread for about 2 minutes on each side, until golden brown. Transfer to a serving platter. Just before serving, top with the tomato mixture.

AVOCADO TOAST

1. In a bowl, stir the avocado together with the olive oil and 1 teaspoon of lemon juice. Season with sea salt. Set aside.

2. In a separate bowl, whisk the tahini with the remaining lemon juice and season with sea salt.

3. Toast another third of the bread slices in a toaster oven until lightly golden brown.

4. Spread the avocado mixture over each piece of toast. Top with a few tomatoes and a pinch of microgreens. Drizzle with the tahini mixture. Season with a dash of togarashi, if using.

AVOCADO TOAST

2 avocados, mashed

1 tablespoon extra-virgin olive oil

juice of 1 lemon, divided

2 tablespoons tahini

12 grape tomatoes, halved

small handful of microgreens

dash of togarashi (optional)

sea salt, to taste

SMOKED SALMON TOAST

4 ounces cream cheese

¼ cup mayonnaise

¼ cup sour cream

4 ounces smoked (not cured) salmon, flaked

¼ teaspoon sea salt

2 tablespoons minced chives

1 teaspoon lemon juice

4 sprigs fresh dill, torn into smaller sprigs

SMOKED SALMON TOAST

1. Combine the cream cheese, mayonnaise, sour cream, salmon, sea salt, chives, and lemon juice until fully mixed (the smoked salmon will remain in pieces).

2. Toast the final third of the bread slices in a toaster oven until lightly golden brown.

3. Spread the salmon mixture over the toasts and top each with a sprig of dill.

Tavern Pretzel Bites and Beer Cheese

SERVES
4 to 6

PREP TIME
15 minutes

COOK TIME
15 minutes

Settle in for some tavern food with these pretzel bites with beer cheese. They'll keep you warm and cozy as you relax and enjoy an evening with friends. Tip: if boiling your own pretzels sounds like too much work, feel free to buy frozen. You may lose some of that classic pretzel taste, but if you're looking for an easy treat, they'll save the day. Mix up your snack table by adding in some Scalded Feta Barbarian Skewers (page 34) or Stuffed Mushrooms with Fresh Island Herbs (page 46) for a balanced selection.

PRETZEL BITES

¼ cup baking soda

1 (12- to 14-ounce) container premade pizza dough

1 egg, beaten with 1 tablespoon water

kosher salt or pretzel salt, to taste

PRETZEL BITES

1. Preheat the oven to 425°F. Bring 2 quarts of water to a boil in a large pot. Add the baking soda.

2. Roll the pizza dough out and cut it into 2-inch pieces. Boil the pizza dough bites for 2 to 3 minutes, or until puffy. Use a spider skimmer or slotted spoon to transfer them to a cooling rack to dry briefly.

3. Line a rimmed baking sheet with parchment paper. Transfer the boiled dough to the cookie sheet, spacing evenly.

4. Brush the tops with a bit of the egg wash. Sprinkle with salt. Bake for 10 to 12 minutes, or until golden brown. Serve with the beer cheese.

BEER CHEESE

1. Combine the butter and flour in a medium saucepan over medium heat. Whisk the flour and butter together to form a paste. Allow it to cook for about 1 minute. Add the onion powder, garlic powder, and smoked paprika.

2. Add in the milk, beer, mustard, and Worcestershire sauce then whisk until the liquid thickens. Remove the pan from the heat. The sauce should not be bubbling; if it's too hot, it will curdle the cheese. Add the cheddar cheese and stir just until melted.

BEER CHEESE

3 tablespoons butter

3 tablespoons all-purpose flour

½ teaspoon onion powder

½ teaspoon garlic powder

½ teaspoon smoked paprika

¾ cup milk

⅔ cup beer (a lager for milder flavor or IPA for more intense flavor)

1 teaspoon Dijon mustard

1 teaspoon Worcestershire sauce

2 cups shredded sharp cheddar cheese

Seaworthy Beef Jerky

This sailor-friendly snack is perfect for Catanians who take advantage of harbors as part of their game-winning strategy. This particular jerky recipe will store in the freezer for ages, or you can keep it in an airtight container up to a few weeks before you plan to serve. It pairs perfectly with sweet or savory snacks, especially trail mixes and Manchego Cheese Crackers (page 31).

MAKES
8 ounces

PREP TIME
10 minutes, plus
2 hours to freeze and
4 hours to marinate

COOK TIME
4 to 5 hours

2 pounds flank steak

¼ cup packed brown sugar

1 cup soy sauce

½ cup Worcestershire sauce

2 teaspoons smoked paprika

2 teaspoons freshly ground black pepper

1 teaspoon red chile flakes

1 teaspoon onion powder

½ teaspoon garlic powder

DF
LF

INSTRUCTIONS

1. Trim the flank steak of any fat and place it in the freezer for 2 hours to firm up. Thinly slice the meat into long, thin strips with the grain.

2. Combine the brown sugar, soy sauce, Worcestershire sauce, paprika, black pepper, red chile flakes, onion powder, and garlic powder in a large zip-top bag. Add the steak strips and turn to coat them in the mixture. Remove excess air from the bag and transfer to the refrigerator to marinate the meat for at least 4 hours, or up to overnight.

3. Remove the meat from the bag and pat dry with paper towels. Transfer to a dehydrator tray and dehydrate for 4 to 5 hours at 165°F. If you don't have a dehydrator, place the beef on a metal drying rack over a baking tray and bake at 200°F, or on your oven's lowest setting, with the oven door propped open by a wooden spoon by an inch or so. The jerky is done when it reaches an internal temperature of 160°F, about 4 hours.

Stuffed Mushrooms with Fresh Island Herbs

SERVES
4 to 6

PREP TIME
10 minutes

COOK TIME
20 minutes

Fresh herbs, cheese, and bread crumbs make the perfect stuffing for fungi you might find along the trail. They don't take long to prepare, either, with just 10 minutes prep time and 20 minutes baking time. They're delicious and hit the spot for savory food lovers. Also relish a hint of sweetness, thanks to that cream cheese.

4 ounces cream cheese

½ cup shredded parmesan

½ cup fresh bread crumbs

1 teaspoon minced fresh thyme

1 tablespoon minced fresh parsley, plus more for garnish

1 clove garlic, minced

½ teaspoon freshly ground black pepper

¼ teaspoon sea salt

1 pound button mushrooms, stems removed, dirt brushed away

INSTRUCTIONS

1. Preheat the oven to 400°F. Line a rimmed baking sheet with parchment paper.

2. Mix the cream cheese, parmesan, bread crumbs, thyme, parsley, garlic, black pepper, and salt in a small mixing bowl until thoroughly integrated.

3. Divide the mixture between the mushrooms and place them on the baking sheet. Bake for 20 minutes, or until the mushrooms are golden brown. Allow to cool for 5 minutes before serving.

Adventurer's Charcuterie Board

For one of the fastest, easiest, and most flavorful "fancy" meals, pull out the cheeses, nuts, and imported deli meats for this tasty spread. Serve with baguette (toasted or untoasted) and crackers, and nibble while you play. Every time you make this charcuterie board, switch out the meats and cheeses, too, to keep it fresh. Toss in some Forest Dweller's Dip (page 21) and the Forager's Veggie Platter (page 20) for a well-rounded meal.

1 cup assorted marinated olives

1 cup Marcona almonds

1 cup prepared hummus

1 (8-ounce) jar gherkins, drained

8 ounces cured meats, such as prosciutto, jamon serrano, soppressata, and coppa

1 small block hard cheese, such as parmesan or Manchego

1 small round soft cheese, such as brie

1 small block tangy cheese, such as goat cheese or feta

1 small wedge of soft cheese like gorgonzola or Camembert

1 cup dried fruit, such as apricots or cherries

1 bunch red grapes, cut into small bunches (5 to 7 grapes each)

16 ounces crackers, of any variety you like

1 baguette, sliced into ½-inch-thick pieces

INSTRUCTIONS

1. Place the olives, almonds, hummus, and gherkins in individual small bowls or ramekins and arrange them on a large cutting board or serving platter.

2. Arrange the meats, cheeses, fruit, and crackers or bread slices around the bowls.

PART II

Food for the Road

Healthy Salads, Hearty Soups, and More Packable Snacks

Over-Knight Oats

Whole-Grain Pancakes

Farmer's Market Berry Yogurt Parfait

Green Garden Smoothie

Traveler's Egg Sandwich

Desert Jelly

Mug of Barley Soup

7-Grain Bread

Caravan Vegetarian Chili

Coastal Chowder

Miner's Hand Pies

Wheat Berry Salad

Fall Harvest Salad

Seafarer's Summer Salad

DICE-ed Caprese Salad

Over-Knight Oats

SERVES
4

PREP TIME
5 minutes, plus
overnight to chill

COOK TIME
1 minute

What better way to start your game day than with a hearty porridge pot of oats? Even better is a batch of Over-Knight Oats, a meal you prep the night before. Load it up with those bananas, nuts, and sweet spices for the perfect wake-up that's kind of like eating a healthier (but equally delicious!) loaf of banana nut bread.

2 cups old-fashioned rolled oats

6 cups water

1 banana, mashed

1 teaspoon ground cinnamon

¼ teaspoon sea salt

1 cup whole milk or dairy-free milk, for serving

½ cup finely chopped pecans, for serving

butter, for serving

brown sugar, for serving

INSTRUCTIONS

1. Place the oats, water, banana, cinnamon, and salt into a nonreactive pot. Stir gently to mix. Refrigerate overnight.

2. Place the pot on the stovetop and bring to a simmer for 1 minute. Serve with milk, pecans, butter, and brown sugar.

Whole-Grain Pancakes

For a healthy, sweet start to the day, whip up some of these whole-grain pancakes. They're loaded with fiber, easy to make, and pair perfectly with an assortment of other breakfast foods you'll love. Add in Farmer's Market Berry Yogurt Parfait (page 58), sizzled sausages, and Cottage Cheese Mini Quiches (page 33) for the perfect spread for the whole settlement.

SERVES
4 to 6

PREP TIME
5 minutes

COOK TIME
15 minutes

1¾ cups whole-wheat pastry flour

2 tablespoons brown sugar, granulated sugar, or sweetener

1½ tablespoons baking powder

½ teaspoon baking soda

½ teaspoon sea salt

1¾ cups milk

3 tablespoons butter, melted, plus more for serving

2 teaspoons vanilla extract

2 large eggs

maple syrup, for serving

INSTRUCTIONS

1. Combine the flour, sugar, baking powder, baking soda, and salt in a large bowl. Stir to mix. Make a well in the center of the ingredients.

2. Add the milk, butter, vanilla, and eggs to the well and whisk until no lumps remain.

3. Heat a large nonstick griddle or pan over medium-high heat. Use a ¼-cup measuring spoon to ladle the pancake batter onto the griddle, leaving ample space between the pancakes (they'll spread out a bit as you pour them).

4. Cook until small bubbles begin to surface in the center of the pancake and the edges are set, about 2 to 3 minutes. Flip and cook for another minute on the second side. Repeat with the remaining batter.

5. Serve immediately with maple syrup and butter, or transfer to a pan in a 200°F oven to keep warm.

Farmer's Market Berry Yogurt Parfait

SERVES
4

PREP TIME
10 minutes

A super-easy, fast, and udder-ly delicious morning meal is the complete Farmer's Market Berry Yogurt Parfait. Layer in your favorite yogurt, granola, fresh fruit, and nuts for a well-rounded repast that takes 10 minutes to prep and keeps you satisfied for hours.

4 cups whole-milk plain yogurt

4 cups granola

4 cups assorted fresh berries, such as raspberries, blueberries, sliced strawberries, or whatever's in season

4 tablespoons chopped toasted pecans

V

INSTRUCTIONS

1. Layer ⅓ cup of yogurt, ⅓ cup of granola, and ⅓ cup of berries in a glass. Repeat these layers for a total of three layers of each ingredient.

2. Top with 1 tablespoon of pecans.

3. Repeat with the remaining ingredients.

Green Garden Smoothie

You can't get any faster and fresher than a smoothie filled with lush greens and fruits. This Green Garden Smoothie is particularly good to take out on the road, as it's packed with nutritious goodies like bananas, spinach (or kale), and lime. The flavors come together for a sweet (but not too sweet) and refreshing on-the-go meal or easy morning breakfast.

SERVES
4

PREP TIME
5 minutes

1 lime, peeled

2 cups orange juice

6 cups spinach or kale (tough ribs removed)

1 cup roughly chopped fresh parsley or cilantro

4 frozen bananas, cut into chunks

INSTRUCTIONS

1. Place all of the ingredients into a high-speed blender. Puree until smooth. Serve immediately.

DID YOU KNOW? In the Netherlands in 2017, the CATAN – Big Game event broke the largest single game record by having 1,096 participants playing CATAN together at the same time.

Traveler's Egg Sandwich

This sandwich offers a full breakfast of eggs, meat, and toast, all in one road-friendly package, making it the perfect hearty way to start your day, no matter what adventure you've got ahead. Eat solo or pair with the Green Garden Smoothie (page 61) for a whole meal, complete with healthy greens.

SERVES
4

PREP TIME
5 minutes

COOK TIME
5 minutes

4 teaspoons butter, divided

4 English muffins

4 to 8 slices sharp cheddar cheese

4 slices prosciutto

4 eggs

freshly ground pepper, to taste

sea salt, to taste

SF

INSTRUCTIONS

1. Heat 2 teaspoons butter in a large skillet and place all halves of the English muffins in the skillet. Add 1 or 2 slices of cheese to just the bottom muffins and toast until the cheese begins to melt. Transfer all the muffins to a plate.

2. Heat the remaining butter in a separate large, nonstick skillet. Fry the eggs for 2 to 3 minutes, or until the whites are set but the yolk is still runny. Season with salt and pepper.

3. To assemble, on each bottom muffin, add a slice of prosciutto then the fried egg, and top with the second half of the English muffin.

4. Wrap each sandwich in a square of parchment paper so that they can be eaten on the go.

Desert Jelly

Unless you've grown up in the desert, you've likely not eaten a lot of prickly pears. This amazing jelly is made from the fruit of the cacti, blended and prepared into the perfect spread for your 7-Grain Bread (page 68) or as a topping for some yogurt or crackers. Add some into your Adventurer's Charcuterie Board (page 48) for an extra-sweet pairing to go with all those cheeses.

MAKES
4 (½-pint) jars

PREP TIME
10 minutes

COOK TIME
1 hour

10 prickly pears

3 to 4 cups granulated sugar

1 to 2 cups lemon juice, ideally from organic lemons

2 teaspoons pectin powder

INSTRUCTIONS

1. Turn on your gas stove (or gas or charcoal grill) and using gloves or tongs, hold each fruit in the flame to burn off the thorns, turning over the fruit to torch all sides. Set each piece of fruit aside in a bowl. **Important:** be very careful not to touch the prickly pears with your bare hands!

2. When cool enough to handle, cut the ends off of the prickly pears and peel them. Chop into 1-inch pieces.

3. Place the fruit into a nonreactive pot and cook over medium heat for 30 to 45 minutes, stirring until the mixture is thick and pulpy. You may need to add water to keep the mixture from sticking.

4. Pass the fruit through a food mill or sieve, pressing with a wooden spoon to extract the most liquid. You should have roughly 4 cups, depending on the size and moisture content of the fruit.

5. For each cup of liquid, use 1 cup of sugar, ½ cup of lemon juice, and ½ teaspoon of pectin powder. Add these ingredients to a clean pot, mixing thoroughly before adding the prickly pear juice, and bring to a simmer for 5 minutes or until the mixture becomes gel-like.

6. Divide the jelly between clean ½ pint jars, cover, and refrigerate for up to 4 months.

Mug of Barley Soup

You can't get much heartier than a hot mug of grain-based soup. It's loaded with veggies, herbs and spices, beef, and, of course, that thick, stick-to-your-ribs barley that will keep you full and satisfied all day long. You'll never go hungry during your departures into the unknown!

2 tablespoons extra-virgin olive oil

2 pounds beef chuck, cut into 2-inch pieces

1 red bell pepper, cored and diced

1 yellow onion, diced

4 cloves garlic, smashed

1 teaspoon dried oregano

pinch of red chile flakes

2 tablespoons tomato paste

1 cup dry red wine

1 quart low-sodium beef broth

1 cup pearl barley

sea salt, to taste

freshly ground black pepper, to taste

INSTRUCTIONS

1. Heat the olive oil in a large cast-iron pot over medium-high heat. Pat the beef cubes dry with paper towels and season with salt and pepper. Sear on all sides until well browned. To get the best sear, you should do this in batches so as not to crowd the pan. Set the beef aside.

2. Add the bell pepper, onion, garlic, oregano, and red chile flakes to the pot and reduce the heat to medium. Cook for 5 to 7 minutes, until the onions begin to soften.

3. Stir in the tomato paste and cook for 1 to 2 minutes to caramelize the sugars.

4. Add the wine and cook for 3 to 4 minutes, scraping up the browned bits from the bottom of the pan.

5. Stir in the beef broth and the beef and any accumulated juices, cover, and simmer for 2 hours, or until the beef is tender but not falling apart.

6. Stir in the pearl barley and cook for another 45 minutes, or until very soft. Season with salt and pepper to taste. Serve in large mugs with crusty bread.

GLUTEN-FREE VARIATION: In step 6, replace the barley with 1 cup of white or red quinoa and cook for 25 minutes, or until soft.

7-Grain Bread

Break bread with your fellow Catanians...literally. You'll need about 3 hours for it to be ready to serve (including rise and bake times), and you'll likely want some butter, jellies, jams, or other favorite toppings to really hit the spot. It uses 7-grain cereal and wheat to load you up with fiber, vitamin E, B vitamins, and phosphorous—all a part of a super-healthy and happy body. It's a great side for your Coastal Chowder (page 74), Caravan Vegetarian Chili (page 71), or any other rich soups.

MAKES
1 loaf

PREP TIME
2 hours

COOK TIME
45 minutes

1¼ cups warm water (110°F to 115°F), divided

1¼ teaspoons active dry yeast

1 egg, whisked, divided

2 tablespoons melted butter

1 teaspoon sea salt

¼ cup honey or maple syrup

2 cups whole wheat flour

2 cups all-purpose flour

⅔ cup 7-grain cereal

oil, for coating

INSTRUCTIONS

1. Combine ¼ cup of warm water and yeast in a small bowl and let sit for 5 minutes.

2. In a separate bowl, combine the yeast mixture with 2 tablespoons of the whisked egg, the melted butter, 1 cup of warm water, salt, and honey or maple syrup. Sift in the whole wheat flour and all-purpose flour. Stir to mix thoroughly. Turn the dough out onto a lightly floured surface. Knead for about 8 minutes, or until the dough is smooth and elastic. If it is too sticky, add a sprinkle of flour, being careful not to add too much flour or to over-knead the dough.

3. When the dough is ready, add the 7-grain cereal and knead just until it's integrated.

4. Coat the inside of a clean bowl with oil and add the dough. Cover the bowl loosely with a damp, clean towel. Place into a somewhat warm location free from breezes. Allow to rise for 1 hour, or until doubled in size. Punch down the dough.

5. Coat the inside of a 9 x 5-inch loaf pan with oil. Place the dough into the loaf pan and cover with an oiled piece of plastic wrap. Allow to rise for 45 minutes, or until doubled again.

6. Preheat the oven to 350°F. Whisk 1 tablespoon of water into the reserved whisked egg. Gently brush the top of the dough with the egg wash. Bake for 45 minutes or until the crust is golden brown and the loaf sounds hollow when tapped. Transfer to a cooling rack until thoroughly cooled.

DID YOU KNOW? There are more than 40 million CATAN products in circulation.

Caravan Vegetarian Chili

Who says chili has to have meat? This vegetarian chili is loaded with savory flavors, spicy add-ins, and plenty of tomatoes, corn, and beans that will fill you and keep you fueled as long as you need to go. Let it simmer even longer than the 40 minutes for a deeper, richer flavor, then serve it up with some Tavern Pretzel Bites and Beer Cheese (page 41) for a super meal no one will forget anytime soon.

SERVES
4 to 6

PREP TIME
10 minutes

COOK TIME
1 hour 10 minutes to
1 hour 25 minutes

2 tablespoons canola oil

1 yellow onion, diced

6 cloves garlic, minced

2 carrots, diced

2 stalks celery, diced

1 jalapeño pepper, cored and minced

1 pint button mushrooms, diced

1 tablespoon ground cumin

2 tablespoons good-quality chili powder

2 (15-ounce) cans diced fire-roasted tomatoes

2 (15-ounce) cans chili beans, mild or hot

1 teaspoon sea salt

1 teaspoon freshly ground pepper

sharp cheddar, shredded, for serving

sour cream, for serving

corn chips, for serving

INSTRUCTIONS

1. Heat the oil in a large pot over medium heat. Add the onion, garlic, carrots, celery, jalapeño, and mushrooms. Cook for about 10 minutes, until the vegetables are soft and begin to brown.

2. Add the cumin and chili powder and cook for 30 to 45 seconds to toast the spices.

3. Add the tomatoes, beans, salt, and pepper. Cook uncovered for 30 minutes, or until thick and fragrant. Serve each bowl with a generous sprinkle of cheddar cheese, a dollop of sour cream, and a side of corn chips.

Coastal Chowder

Building on coastal intersections might not reward you with a resource after every roll, but you'll see the fruits of your labors via maritime trade. This thick, creamy chowder packed with herbs, potatoes, and seafood offers a delicious and immediate reward.

SERVES
4 to 6

PREP TIME
10 minutes

COOK TIME
25 minutes

2 tablespoons butter

1 onion, diced

2 stalks celery, diced

2 tablespoons minced fresh parsley

1 teaspoon dried thyme

¼ teaspoon red chile flakes

1 pound Yukon gold potatoes, diced

2 tablespoons all-purpose or gluten-free flour blend

½ cup dry white wine

2 quarts chicken stock

1 pound fresh fish, cut into 2-inch pieces

8 ounces bay scallops

2 pounds clams or mussels, scrubbed and debearded

1 cup heavy cream

SF

INSTRUCTIONS

1. Melt the butter in a large pot over medium heat. Cook the onion, celery, parsley, thyme, red chile flakes, and potatoes for 10 minutes, until the vegetables begin to soften.

2. Stir in the flour and cook for another minute or until no lumps remain.

3. Add the wine and cook for 2 minutes, until most of the liquid has evaporated. Stir in the chicken stock and bring to a simmer.

4. Add the fish, scallops, clams or mussels, and heavy cream. Cover and continue cooking for another 8 to 10 minutes, or until the fish is cooked through and all of the shellfish have opened. Discard any shellfish that haven't opened.

Miner's Hand Pies

If you're not familiar with pasties—a traditional hand-held meal dating back to the mid-1800s in the Cornish mining industry—you are now. These delicious pocket sandwiches pay homage to the hills and mountains of Catan. Loaded with veggies, beef, and herbs and seasonings, they take very little time to make. In under an hour, you'll have a complete, balanced meal you can eat on the go or plate for the whole gathering to snag as needed.

1 pound cooked beef roast, such as slow-simmered beef au jus

½ cup frozen peas, defrosted

½ cup frozen diced carrots, defrosted

1 cup frozen diced potatoes (hash browns), defrosted

1 tablespoon minced fresh rosemary

1 tablespoon minced fresh parsley

2 tablespoons all-purpose flour

½ teaspoon sea salt

½ teaspoon freshly ground black pepper

2 (17.3-ounce) packages frozen puff pastry sheets, thawed

1 egg, whisked with 1 tablespoon water

SF

INSTRUCTIONS

1. Preheat the oven to 400°F. Line a baking sheet with parchment paper.

2. Combine the beef, peas, carrots, potatoes, rosemary, parsley, flour, salt, and pepper in a mixing bowl. Set aside.

3. Cut each puff pastry sheet into four 5-inch squares. Place four of the puff pastry squares on the baking sheet. Divide the filling between the pastry squares, leaving about 1 inch of margin around the edges of the squares. Brush the edges with the egg wash. Place another pastry square atop the filling, pressing gently to seal the edges. Make a small cut in the top of each hand pie to allow steam to escape.

4. Bake for 20 to 25 minutes, or until golden brown. Allow to cool for 10 minutes before serving.

Wheat Berry Salad

Smart Catanians use every resource at their disposal, especially when it comes to grain! Enjoy grain at its most basic with wheat berries: whole grain kernels before refinement that are loaded with fiber, protein, and iron. They're perfect to bulk up your salads with flavor, nutrition, and satiety value. Pair the salad with your favorite sandwich for extra fiber, or add as a side with your Great Hall Rack of Lamb (page 107) or Smoked Game Legs (page 95).

SERVES
4 to 6

PREP TIME
10 minutes

COOK TIME
30 to 45 minutes

1 cup dry wheat berries

3 cups water, plus more as needed

¼ cup red wine vinegar

¼ cup extra-virgin olive oil

½ teaspoon sea salt

1 teaspoon sugar

1 cup roughly chopped fresh basil

4 green onions, white and green parts, thinly sliced on a bias

2 cups fresh black cherries, pitted and halved

INSTRUCTIONS

1. Rinse and drain the wheat berries.

2. Bring the water to a boil in a large pot with a generous pinch of salt. Simmer uncovered for 30 to 45 minutes for soft wheat berries (double time for hard wheat berries). Rinse under cool water and drain.

3. In a large bowl, whisk the vinegar, oil, salt, and sugar. Add the cooled wheat berries and stir to mix thoroughly.

4. Gently stir in the basil, green onions, and cherries.

GLUTEN-FREE VARIATION: Replace the wheat berries with 1 cup of black or brown rice. Cook in 2 cups of water for 25 to 30 minutes. Rinse and drain.

Fall Harvest Salad

Celebrate the change of seasons and abundant resources with this hearty and flavorful autumnal salad that features seasonal squash as the centerpiece. Prepare ahead for an easy meal or make a same-day feast of it.

SERVES
4 to 6

PREP TIME
10 minutes

COOK TIME
30 minutes

1 winter squash, such as kabocha, unpeeled, cut into 2-inch pieces

4 tablespoons extra-virgin olive oil, divided

1 teaspoon ground cinnamon

freshly ground black pepper, to taste

1 cup black rice

2 cups arugula

¼ cup minced fresh parsley

½ cup roughly chopped toasted pecans

1 cup dried cranberries

¼ cup balsamic vinegar

1 tablespoon maple syrup

sea salt, to taste

INSTRUCTIONS

1. Preheat the oven to 400°F. Toss the squash in 2 tablespoons of the oil and the cinnamon, and season with salt and pepper. Spread onto a rimmed baking sheet lined with parchment paper. Roast for 30 minutes, or until gently browned at the edges and tender.

2. While the squash cooks, place the black rice into a small saucepan with 2 cups of water and a generous pinch of salt. Bring to a simmer, cover, and cook for 25 minutes, or until just tender. Drain.

3. Toss the cooked squash with the cooked rice, arugula, parsley, pecans, and cranberries.

4. In a separate bowl, whisk together the balsamic vinegar, maple syrup, and the remaining 2 tablespoons of olive oil, and season with salt and pepper. Pour the dressing over the salad and toss gently to mix.

Seafarer's Summer Salad

Not all salads use leafy greens—and this Seafarer's Summer Salad is the perfect example of that. Combining fruits and seasonings with olive oil topping, the salad will last a good long while as you make your way across the Seven Seas—or the game table. It's packed with all those ingredients needed to keep your immune system healthy (no scurvy here!) and your belly happy.

2 large ripe avocados, pitted, halved, and sliced into 12 wedges total

1 large orange, ends sliced

1 oro blanco grapefruit or pink grapefruit, ends sliced

pinch of red chili flakes

sea salt, to taste

extra-virgin olive oil, to taste

INSTRUCTIONS

1. Arrange the avocado slices on a serving platter.

2. Supreme the orange. To do so, stand the orange on one of the cut ends and slice off the peel. Slice between the membranes to remove the orange segments. Repeat the same process with the grapefruit. Arrange the citrus slices on the serving platter with the avocado slices.

3. Season with the red chili flakes, salt, and olive oil.

DICE-ed Caprese Salad

Shake up a traditional caprese salad with this fresh diced take on a classic. The structured preparation not only adds an inspired game theme to your table, but also makes for a perfect side salad or topping for your baguettes and crackers. Make sure to use fresh basil instead of dried for a zesty, fresh flavor that's to die for!

SERVES
4 to 6

PREP TIME
15 minutes

2 (4-ounce) balls fresh mozzarella, cut into ½-inch pieces

2 medium-large vine-ripe tomatoes, cut into ½-inch pieces

2 tablespoons good-quality balsamic vinegar

2 tablespoons extra-virgin olive oil

handful of fresh basil, minced

sea salt, to taste

freshly ground pepper, to taste

INSTRUCTIONS

1. Mix all of the ingredients in a serving bowl, seasoning with the salt and pepper to taste.

2. Set aside for 5 minutes to allow the flavors to come together.

PART III
Adventurer's Feast
Main Dishes, Hearty Suppers, and More Celebratory Meals

Robber's Discard Delight

Chicken under a Brick

Beer-Grilled Chicken

Smoked Game Legs

Brick Smash Burger

Tavern Ale Pie

Traditional Shepherd's Pie

Lamb Bolognese

Great Hall Rack of Lamb

Pasture-Fed Lamb Kebabs

Cedar-Plank Grilled Salmon

Harbormaster's Fish and Chips

Iron-Skillet Shrimp and Blackened Corn

Brick-Oven Pizza

Forest Mushroom Risotto

Fire-Roasted Veggie Grain Bowl

Traditional German Fried Potatoes

Field Corn Grits

Harvest Dinner Rolls

Charred Summer Vegetables

Crispy Cast-Iron Brussels Sprouts

Robber's Discard Delight

Nothing feels better than using every single resource you have—wasting nothing. The Robber's Discard Delight is the perfect way to use all those leftovers from the fridge, from potatoes or fries to ham, bacon, or chicken. Toss in the eggs, bell pepper, and seasoning, and not only have you saved the food, but you've also saved the day with a delicious meal. Plus, if you have any other leftovers lying around (meats and veggies!), you can toss them in and put them to good use, too.

SERVES
4 to 6

PREP TIME
5 minutes

COOK TIME
12 minutes

3 tablespoons canola oil, divided

1 green bell pepper, cored and finely diced

2 cups leftover french fries, baked potatoes, or roasted potatoes, roughly chopped

½ cup diced ham or cooked bacon or 1 cup chopped rotisserie chicken

4 eggs

sea salt, to taste

freshly ground pepper, to taste

INSTRUCTIONS

1. Heat 2 tablespoons of the canola oil in a large skillet over high heat. Sauté the bell pepper for 2 to 3 minutes, until it begins to brown.

2. Add the potatoes and meat, and cook for another 2 to 3 minutes, until all of the ingredients are just heated through. Transfer them to individual serving dishes.

3. Heat the remaining tablespoon of canola oil in the skillet. Fry the eggs to your desired level of doneness. Season with salt and pepper and place them atop the hash.

Chicken under a Brick

Everyone knows that one Brick and one Lumber make a road. But what about two bricks and four chicken thighs? That's the beginnings of an amazingly delicious, yet simple, main dish. Add a lemon, oven, and aluminum foil, and you're all set. This recipe is fast and easy, and will add some victory points to your cooking game.

SERVES
4

PREP TIME
5 minutes

COOK TIME
15 minutes

4 boneless, skin-on chicken thighs (ask your butcher to remove the bones for you)

extra-virgin olive oil, for coating

2 lemons, halved

sea salt, to taste

freshly ground pepper, to taste

INSTRUCTIONS

1. Preheat the oven to 425°F. Wrap two bricks in aluminum foil.

2. Season the chicken on all sides with salt and pepper.

3. Heat a large cast-iron skillet over high heat for about 2 to 3 minutes, or until very hot. Add enough olive oil to coat the bottom of the pan. Place the chicken skin-side down into the hot pan and place the lemons cut-side down into the pan. Immediately top the chicken with the bricks or, if you don't have any, a second cast-iron skillet. Carefully transfer the pan to the oven (oven mitts will be very helpful here.)

4. Bake for 10 to 12 minutes, or until the chicken is cooked to an internal temperature of 155°F (it will continue to cook after being removed from the oven).

5. Transfer the chicken to a serving platter and squeeze the roasted lemon halves over it.

Beer-Grilled Chicken

The perfect cook-while-you-play meal, this Beer-Grilled Chicken hits all the high points of flavor. Using smoked paprika and other dried spices, a whole chicken, and a beer can, this recipe is a unique take on chugging one back on a casual night. Drink up before cooking (or while you play) and enjoy the tasty grilled chicken in about one and a half hours, thanks to the unique use of the beer can that helps cook this bird.

SERVES
4 to 6

PREP TIME
10 minutes

COOK TIME
1 to 1½ hours

1 tablespoon smoked paprika

1 teaspoon dried thyme

1 teaspoon garlic powder

1 teaspoon sea salt

1 teaspoon freshly ground black pepper

1 (3- to 4-pound) whole chicken

2 tablespoons canola oil

1 (12-ounce) can beer, about ¼ cup poured out (or drank!)

SF

INSTRUCTIONS

1. Combine the paprika, thyme, garlic powder, salt, and pepper in a small bowl.

2. Pat the chicken dry with paper towels and then coat with the oil. Season inside and out with the spice mix.

3. Place the beer can in the center of a baking dish (you won't be using this dish on the grill; it's just for transport). Place the chicken carefully onto the beer can with the breasts facing up.

4. Carefully transfer the chicken to the hot grill, cover, and cook for 1 to 1½ hours, or until the chicken reaches an internal temperature of 155°F (it will continue to cook after being removed from the heat).

5. Remove the beer can and set the chicken on a serving platter. Allow to rest for at least 10 minutes before serving.

Smoked Game Legs

One of the most popular menu items at any Renaissance faire, smoked turkey legs are the perfect main for a historical mood meal. The zesty brine needs a night to do its magic, and the smoker (or grill!) will take a few hours to smoke them up right, but when you take that first bite, you'll know it was worth the wait.

SERVES
4

PREP TIME
5 minutes, plus
8 hours to brine

COOK TIME
3 to 3½ hours

1 quart cold water, divided

½ cup brown sugar

½ cup kosher salt

1 tablespoon peppercorns

1 cup apple cider vinegar

4 turkey legs

INSTRUCTIONS

1. Combine 1 cup of the water, the brown sugar, and the salt in a heatproof container. Microwave on high for 1 to 2 minutes. Stir to dissolve the sugar and salt.

2. Add this mixture to the remaining water and stir in the peppercorns and vinegar.

3. Place the turkey legs in 2 gallon-size zip-top bags (two in each) and pour about half of the brine into each bag. Seal carefully, place into a baking dish, and transfer to the refrigerator. Allow to sit in the brine for at least 8 hours or overnight.

4. Remove the turkey legs from the brine and pat dry.

5. Smoke the turkey for 3 to 3½ hours, or until it reaches an internal temperature of 165°F.

   a. Using a smoker: Prepare a smoker with applewood chips to cook at 250°F. Place the turkey legs into the smoker.

   b. Using a gas grill: Soak 2 cups of applewood chips. Using all of the burners, heat the gas grill to 500°F. If you have a smoker box, turn off all but the side burner under the smoker box. Place the chips into the smoker box and close the lid of the box and the grill. Wait until smoke emerges from the grill. (If you don't have a smoker box, place the chips into a large square of aluminum foil and make a loose packet. Place this over the lit burner, close the lid of the grill, and wait until smoke emerges.) Lower the heat under the smoker box or foil packet so that the chips smolder slowly.

Brick Smash Burger

If you love unique cooking utensils, this Brick Smash Burger is your new favorite dish. A crucial resource will help you make the crispiest and juiciest burgers of your life. Follow the instructions carefully to keep the perfect texture for your smash burger and serve up with your favorite toppings and condiments. For a balanced meal, serve alongside the Fall Harvest Salad (page 81).

SERVES
4

PREP TIME
10 minutes

COOK TIME
10 minutes

1½ pounds 80 percent lean ground beef

½ cup mayonnaise

1 teaspoon yellow mustard

1 teaspoon hot sauce

1 teaspoon Worcestershire sauce (optional)

1 tablespoon butter, softened

4 brioche buns

4 slices cheddar cheese

½ red onion, thinly sliced

½ head iceberg lettuce, thinly sliced

1 beefsteak tomato, thinly sliced

sea salt, to taste

SF

INSTRUCTIONS

1. Portion the beef into 8 equal balls. Return them to the refrigerator so they remain cold. This is very important to keep them juicy during the cooking process.

2. Whisk the mayonnaise, mustard, hot sauce, and Worcestershire sauce, if using, in a small bowl. Set aside.

3. Heat a large cast-iron skillet or griddle over medium-high heat.

4. Spread the butter onto the buns and toast for 1 to 2 minutes, until just golden. Set aside.

5. Working quickly, place 4 of the portions of ground beef onto the hot pan. Immediately top with a square of parchment paper and flatten with a brick or the flat side of a meat cleaver. Season with sea salt and top with 1 to 2 teaspoons of the sauce.

6. Flip the burgers after they've cooked for about 2 minutes on the first side and are well browned. Add a slice of cheese on top and cook for 1 minute on the second side. Repeat with the remaining patties.

7. Divide the cooked burgers between the toasted buns and top with more sauce, red onion, lettuce, tomato, and the remaining buns. Serve immediately.

VEGAN VARIATION: Use 1½ pounds Impossible Burger Made from Plants in place of the beef. Swap the mayonnaise for vegan mayo, use a vegan Worcestershire sauce or omit, and use a vegan cheddar.

DID YOU KNOW? CATAN exists in more than 40 languages.

Tavern Ale Pie

For a traditional meal, this Tavern Ale Pie will hit the spot. Using bacon, brisket, mushrooms, fresh herbs and veggies, and dark ale, this hearty pie will satisfy all those hungry stomachs looking for something to keep them filled and strong. It's the perfect piece for a long evening of fun and games.

SERVES
6 to 8

PREP TIME
15 minutes

COOK TIME
3 to 3½ hours

4 strips bacon, about 2 ounces, cut into pieces

2½ pounds brisket, cut into 2-inch pieces

1 cup diced cremini mushrooms

1 cup diced onions

1 cup diced carrots

1 clove garlic, smashed

2 thyme sprigs

1 bay leaf

11 to 12 ounces dark ale or stout

1 tablespoon brown sugar

1 puff pastry crust

sea salt, to taste

freshly ground pepper, to taste

DF

INSTRUCTIONS

1. Preheat the oven to 325°F.

2. In a large cast-iron skillet, cook the bacon over medium-low heat until it renders most of its fat. Transfer it to a separate dish.

3. Pat the brisket dry with paper towels and season generously with salt and pepper. Sear it in batches in the bacon fat.

4. After searing the beef, remove it from the skillet and pour out all but 2 tablespoons of the fat. In the same skillet, cook the mushrooms, onion, carrots, garlic, thyme, and bay leaf for about 7 to 8 minutes, or until the vegetables are soft. Stir in the beer and cook for about 2 minutes, until it reduces slightly. Stir in the brown sugar.

5. Return the brisket and any accumulated juices to the skillet. Cover and cook in the oven for 2½ to 3 hours, or until the meat is very tender. Remove from the oven, remove the thyme sprigs and bay leaf, and stir in the bacon.

6. Cut the puff pastry crust so that it fits into the skillet. Remove the lid and carefully top the meat with the pastry. Return to the oven for 12 minutes, or until the pastry is puffy and golden.

Traditional Shepherd's Pie

Pies aren't just desserts. In fact, many of the best pies are hearty meals unto themselves, like the traditional shepherd's pie full of meat, veggies, and potatoes. Prepare the ingredients in just 20 minutes, then stick it in the oven for a complete meal in less than an hour. Ground lamb would be the most "on theme" for your next CATAN game night.

SERVES
4 to 6

PREP TIME
20 minutes

COOK TIME
45 minutes

1 tablespoon canola oil

1 yellow onion, finely diced

2 carrots, finely diced

1 celery stalk, finely diced

¼ cup minced fresh parsley

1 teaspoon minced fresh thyme

1 pound 80 percent lean ground lamb or ground beef

freshly ground pepper, to taste

1 tablespoon tomato paste

½ cup dry red wine

6 cups prepared mashed potatoes (use instant potato flakes)

sea salt, to taste

GF

SF

INSTRUCTIONS

1. Preheat the oven to 350°F.

2. Heat a large cast-iron skillet over medium-high heat. Add the oil, onion, carrots, celery, parsley, thyme, and a generous pinch of sea salt. Cook for 5 to 7 minutes, until the vegetables are soft. Push them to the edges of the pan.

3. Crumble the meat into the center of the pan. Cook until beginning to brown, about 5 minutes.

4. Season with salt and pepper.

5. Add the tomato paste and cook for 1 minute to caramelize the sugars.

6. Add the red wine and simmer for 2 minutes.

7. Spread the mashed potatoes over the top of the meat mixture. Bake for 30 minutes.

VEGAN VARIATION: Use 1 pound Impossible Burger Made from Plants or Beyond Burger or 2 cups cooked black lentils in place of the beef. Use vegan butter and milk when preparing the mashed potatoes.

Lamb Bolognese

A savory pasta dish with rustic vibes, this Lamb Bolognese is the perfect meal to set the mood for a cozy night. It's fairly easy to prepare, loaded with lamb, veggies, and cheese, and the active work time is just 15 minutes. And for that intriguing flavor touch, it uses freshly ground nutmeg to really send your taste buds into new worlds.

SERVES
4 to 6

PREP TIME
15 minutes

COOK TIME
2⅓ to 3⅓ hours

2 tablespoons butter

1 small yellow onion, diced

2 stalks celery, diced

1 carrot, peeled and diced

1½ pounds ground lamb

freshly ground pepper, to taste

2 cups whole milk

1 whole nutmeg clove, or a pinch of ground nutmeg

1½ cups dry white wine

1 (28-ounce) can plum tomatoes, with their juices, hand crushed

pasta, for serving

1 (4-ounce) block Pecorino Romano

flat-leaf parsley, roughly chopped, for serving

sea salt, to taste

INSTRUCTIONS

1. Melt the butter in a large, heavy pot over medium heat. Cook the onion, celery, and carrot for 2 to 3 minutes, until beginning to soften.

2. Add the ground lamb and season generously with salt and pepper. Cook for about 2 to 3 minutes.

3. Add the milk and continue cooking for another 5 minutes, or until it has cooked down almost completely.

4. Use a Microplane grater to add a few gratings of fresh nutmeg. Or, if using pre-ground nutmeg, add just a pinch.

5. Add the white wine, using a wooden spoon to scrape up any browned bits from the bottom of the pan. Again, cook for about 5 minutes or until the wine has all but cooked down completely. Stir in the tomatoes and bring to a gentle simmer for 2 to 3 hours, adding a splash of water here and there as needed to keep the sauce from drying out.

6. Toss with cooked pasta and top with shavings of Pecorino Romano and fresh parsley.

SF

Great Hall Rack of Lamb

A sweet and savory meal fit for a king, the Great Hall Rack of Lamb is the perfect meal for a gathering of 4 to 6 players. The flavorful dish combines unique flavors you might not typically think of together (mint, golden raisins, yogurt) to create a decadent yet savory feast. Pair with your favorite grown-up beverages and a veggie side of Stuffed Mushrooms with Fresh Island Herbs (page 46) for a zesty and complete feast. Queue up the trumpets on your party playlist when you present this majestic main dish.

SERVES
4 to 6

PREP TIME
15 minutes, plus
40 minutes to rest

COOK TIME
25 minutes

2 tablespoons minced fresh rosemary

¼ cup plus 1 tablespoon extra-virgin olive oil, divided

2 tablespoons minced garlic, divided

1 teaspoon sea salt, plus more to taste

1 teaspoon freshly ground pepper, plus more to taste

2 racks of lamb, frenched (about 2 pounds each)

½ cup whole-milk yogurt

2 tablespoons tahini

1 to 2 teaspoons lemon juice

pinch sumac (optional)

¼ cup golden raisins

2 tablespoons fresh mint leaves

GF
SF

107

INSTRUCTIONS

1. Combine the rosemary, ¼ cup of the olive oil, all but 1 teaspoon of the garlic, salt, and pepper in a small bowl. Coat the lamb racks in the mixture and place on a rimmed baking sheet. Allow to rest in the mixture for at least 30 minutes (up to 4 hours in the refrigerator).

2. Preheat the oven to 450°F. Roast for 15 minutes, then rotate the pan and roast for another 10 minutes for medium-rare. Allow the lamb to rest for 10 minutes before carving between the bones.

3. While the lamb cooks, whisk the yogurt, reserved 1 teaspoon of garlic, 1 tablespoon of olive oil, tahini, and lemon juice in a small bowl. Season with salt and pepper, adding more lemon juice if desired.

4. Serve the lamb on a large serving platter, garnished with sumac, raisins, and mint leaves, with the yogurt tahini sauce on the side.

Pasture-Fed Lamb Kebabs

SERVES
4 to 6

PREP TIME
5 minutes, plus
30 minutes to marinate

COOK TIME
10 minutes

A quick, tasty meal that can't be beat is the Pasture-Fed Lamb Kebabs. They're easy to prepare ahead of time but fast enough that you won't mind making them at dinner time. Just be sure to give yourself that 30-minute window for marinating the kebab meat. It takes just a few minutes to skewer everything and only 10 minutes to cook. Tip: make the yogurt sauce while the kebabs grill.

LAMB KEBABS

½ teaspoon cayenne pepper

⅛ teaspoon ground cinnamon

1 teaspoon garlic powder

1 teaspoon sea salt

1 teaspoon ground black pepper

2 tablespoons extra-virgin olive oil

2 pounds lamb loin, trimmed and cut into 1-inch pieces

YOGURT SAUCE

1 cup whole-milk, plain yogurt

1 teaspoon minced garlic

1 tablespoon lemon juice

1 tablespoon minced fresh mint

¼ teaspoon sea salt

INSTRUCTIONS

1. Combine the cayenne, cinnamon, garlic powder, salt, pepper, and olive oil in a shallow dish. Place the lamb shoulder into the mixture and turn to coat it in the spices. Set aside to marinate for at least 30 minutes or up to a day.

2. Remove the lamb from the marinade and thread onto metal or bamboo skewers.

3. Heat a grill or grill pan to medium-high heat. Cook the lamb for 3 to 4 minutes on each side, or until cooked through to your desired level of doneness.

4. To make the yogurt sauce, combine the yogurt, garlic, lemon juice, mint, and sea salt. Serve on the side.

DID YOU KNOW? CATAN is an island analogous to the Azores in terms of landscape and geography.

Cedar-Plank Grilled Salmon

Collecting plenty of Lumber is crucial to play CATAN, but you just need one piece of cedar for this savory, melt-in-your mouth dish. Cooking atop a cedar plank lends a natural fragrant smokiness to whatever's being cooked. This Cedar-Plank Grilled Salmon is that much better because of that woody flavoring. Be sure to soak the cedar plank (it really isn't optional!) for best results and serve with a light veggie side, salad, or tropical fruit salad for the best flavor combination possible.

SERVES
4 to 6

PREP TIME
5 minutes, plus
1 hour to soak

COOK TIME
8 to 10 minutes

1 large untreated cedar plank

2 cups dry white wine

1 (1½- to 2-pound) salmon fillet, skin removed

1 tablespoon melted butter

freshly ground black pepper, to taste

1 teaspoon lemon zest

1 tablespoon minced dill

2 teaspoons minced garlic

sea salt, to taste

INSTRUCTIONS

1. About an hour before grilling, soak the cedar plank in a mixture of 2 cups of white wine and 1 cup of water.

2. Preheat a gas grill to medium. Place the salmon onto the cedar plan and top with the melted butter. Season generously with sea salt and pepper, and sprinkle with the lemon zest, dill, and garlic.

3. Place the cedar plank onto the grill and cook for 8 to 10 minutes, or until the salmon appears done on the outside but is still deep pink on the inside. It will continue cooking after you remove it from the grill. Allow to rest for about 2 minutes on the cedar plank before serving.

Harbormaster's Fish and Chips

Building seaside settlements and cities isn't always smooth sailing, but the reward of a bustling commerce site makes the road(s) to get there well worth it. Same goes for this recipe. The extra work really pays off in the deep flavors in the chips (fries) and battered fish you'll want to eat time and again. It's the perfect treat for a game night, party, or when you just need some good old-fashioned comfort food.

SERVES
4 to 6

PREP TIME
15 minutes

COOK TIME
25 minutes

CHIPS

1. Preheat the oven to 400°F. Line a baking sheet with parchment paper.

2. To make the chips, cut the potatoes into ¼-inch-thick shoestrings. Place them into a bowl and coat them thoroughly in canola oil. Spread them on the parchment-lined baking sheet and bake for 20 to 25 minutes, or until browned and crispy. Sprinkle the fries with sea salt to taste.

CHIPS

1 pound russet potatoes

2 tablespoons canola oil

sea salt, to taste

FISH

1 cup all-purpose flour

1 teaspoon baking powder

1 teaspoon sea salt

½ teaspoon black pepper

1 cup cold beer

vegetable oil, for frying

2 pounds fresh cod or halibut, cut into 2 x 4-inch strips

1 cup tartar sauce, for serving

lemon wedges, for serving

FISH

1. To make the fish, in a mixing bowl, combine the flour, baking powder, sea salt, and black pepper.

2. Gradually pour the cold beer into the mixing bowl, whisking continuously until a smooth batter forms.

3. In a deep frying pan or pot, heat the vegetable oil to 350°F.

4. When the oil is at temperature, dip each piece of fish into the batter, coating it completely.

5. One at a time, gently lower the battered fish pieces into the hot oil, being careful not to overcrowd the pan.

6. Fry the fish for 4 to 5 minutes, flipping it over once halfway through, until the batter is crispy and golden brown.

7. Use a slotted spoon to remove the fish from the oil and drain on a rack placed on a rimmed baking sheet.

8. Serve the fish hot, alongside the baked chips and tartar sauce. Squeeze lemon juice over the fish before serving.

Iron-Skillet Shrimp and Blackened Corn

SERVES
4 to 6

PREP TIME
10 minutes

COOK TIME
10 minutes

If you've never eaten blackened foods before, you're going to love this slightly charred centerpiece on your menu. The sizzling skillet shrimp draw all the attention, but it's those corncobs that steal the show. It won't take you long to make either portion of the meal—just 20 minutes total, including prep time. Tip: preheat the grill after you gather the ingredients to get a head start on time if a wagonload of guests is fast approaching.

1 stick butter, softened

¼ cup minced fresh basil

1 teaspoon minced garlic

zest and juice of 1 lime

2 pounds peeled jumbo shrimp

4 ears corn

1 tablespoon canola oil

INSTRUCTIONS

1. Mix the butter, basil, garlic, and lime zest and juice in a small bowl. Set aside two tablespoons of this mixture.

2. Coat the shrimp in the basil butter and set aside.

3. Preheat a gas grill to high. Coat the corn in the oil and place it onto the heated grill grates, turning as needed to get an even char, about 10 minutes total.

4. Place a cast-iron skillet on one side of the grill and heat until it is very hot. Cook the shrimp for about 1 to 2 minutes on each side, or until they begin to form a C-curve and become opaque. They will continue cooking after you remove them from the heat.

5. Baste the corn with the reserved 2 tablespoons of the basil butter and serve alongside the shrimp.

Brick-Oven Pizza

Looking for a meal that can please even the pickiest of Catanians? You can't go wrong with pizza. Better yet, a stone-fired pizza with that hint of char only a brick or stone could add. The nice thing about this recipe is that you can make your own dough (gluten-free upgrade!) or grab some premade dough for a quicker prep time. The toppings recommended make for a meaty, cheesy delight, but you can always change it up each time you serve it, or make it vegetarian or vegan friendly, as needed.

SERVES
4

PREP TIME
10 minutes

COOK TIME
4 to 5 minutes

16 ounces pizza dough

1 cup marinara sauce

4 ounces Pecorino Romano

8 ounces mozzarella

8 ounces cooked Italian sausage, crumbled

4 ounces cooked pancetta or ham

¼ cup minced fresh basil

SF

INSTRUCTIONS

1. Place the oven rack on the top third of the oven. Place a pizza stone on the rack and preheat the oven to 500°F.

2. Spread a sheet of parchment paper onto a pizza pan or cookie sheet without a rim (this will allow you to slide it easily into the oven).

3. Use your hands to stretch the dough until it reaches the desired size. Spread this onto the parchment paper. Top with the marinara sauce, Pecorino Romano, mozzarella, sausage, and ham.

4. Using oven mitts, carefully slide the dough from the baking sheet onto the pizza stone. Immediately turn on the broiler to high. Cook for 4 to 5 minutes, or until the pizza is browned and the cheese is bubbling. Turn off the broiler and carefully remove the pizza from the oven using a pizza peel, or transfer it back onto the pan.

5. Sprinkle with the fresh basil and serve.

Forest Mushroom Risotto

Why did the mushroom merchant get invited to all the parties? Because he was a *fun-ghi*! Okay, but seriously, this mushroom risotto dish is the perfect choice for a cozy evening with friends and family who love a bit of cheese and a lot of mushrooms.

SERVES
4 to 6

PREP TIME
10 minutes

COOK TIME
30 minutes

2 ounces wild mushrooms

1 pint crimini mushrooms, rinsed and sliced

2 tablespoons butter, divided

1 tablespoon canola oil

½ yellow onion, minced

3 tablespoons dry sherry (optional)

1½ cups arborio or short-grain rice

8 cups chicken or vegetable stock

2 sprigs thyme

½ teaspoon lemon zest

1 cup frozen peas, thawed

¼ cup fresh roughly chopped flat-leaf parsley

½ cup freshly grated parmesan

INSTRUCTIONS

1. Soak the wild mushrooms in 1 cup of hot water for at least 10 minutes, or until softened. Rinse well to remove any grit. Roughly chop the mushrooms. Pour the soaking liquid through a coffee filter and reserve it.

2. Heat 1 tablespoon of the butter and oil in a large skillet over medium heat. Cook the onion for 3 to 5 minutes, or until beginning to soften. Push it to the sides of the pan. Add another tablespoon of the butter. Sear the crimini mushrooms on each side until well browned. Deglaze the pan with the sherry, if using.

3. Add the rice to the pan and cook for 1 to 2 minutes, or until it smells toasty and has absorbed some of the fat from the pan. Add 1 cup of the stock, the wild mushrooms, the strained soaking liquid, the thyme, and the lemon zest, and stir with a wooden spoon until all of the liquid is absorbed. Repeat with the remaining stock, stirring constantly. This process will take at least 20 minutes and you may have some stock left over. The risotto is done when the rice is cooked through but still has a nice bite to it.

4. Stir in the peas, parsley, and parmesan. Remove the thyme sprigs. Divide between your trading companions and enjoy!

Fire-Roasted Veggie Grain Bowl

SERVES
4 to 6

PREP TIME
15 minutes

COOK TIME
25 minutes

Quinoa might not be the primary grain of the field hexes of CATAN, but it's a great real-life seed for healthy dishes that taste amazing while being packed with protein. This grain bowl combines quinoa, fresh veggies, corn, black beans, cheese, and many other favorite ingredients to make a complete meal.

1½ cups quinoa

1 tablespoon canola oil

½ yellow onion, diced

3 cloves garlic, smashed

1 green bell pepper, cored and diced

1 (10-ounce) jar charred piquillo peppers, drained and roughly chopped

1 (15-ounce) can diced fire-roasted tomatoes, drained

1 (15-ounce) can black beans, drained

freshly ground black pepper, to taste

1 tablespoon adobo sauce (from jarred chipotles)

1 clove garlic, minced

1 tablespoon lime juice

1 teaspoon sugar

½ cup sour cream

1 cup fire-roasted frozen corn, thawed

¼ cup roughly chopped cilantro

4 ounces cotija cheese, crumbled

sea salt, to taste

INSTRUCTIONS

1. Place the quinoa into a medium pot with 3 cups of water and a generous pinch of sea salt. Bring to a simmer, cover, and cook for 15 to 18 minutes, or until all of the liquid is absorbed. Fluff with a fork.

2. Heat the oil in a large skillet over medium-high heat. Cook the onion, garlic, and bell pepper for 5 to 7 minutes, or until soft, being careful not to burn the garlic. Add the piquillo peppers, tomatoes, and black beans. Season with salt and pepper. Bring to a simmer.

3. In a separate container, whisk together the adobo sauce, garlic, lime juice, sugar, and sour cream to make your chipotle lime crema.

4. Divide the quinoa, beans, and corn between serving bowls. Top with the cilantro, cotija, and chipotle lime crema.

Traditional German Fried Potatoes

Pairing perfectly with any meaty dish like Great Hall Rack of Lamb (page 107) or Chicken under a Brick (page 91), Traditional German Fried Potatoes are a flavorful choice using Yukon potatoes and bacon. The dish honors the German origin of the game CATAN while providing you with a delicious side for practically any meal.

SERVES
4 to 6

PREP TIME
15 minutes

COOK TIME
30 minutes

4 slices bacon, cut into ½-inch pieces

1½ pounds Yukon gold potatoes, cut into 1-inch pieces

freshly ground black pepper, to taste

2 tablespoons apple cider vinegar

¾ cup chicken stock

1 tablespoon all-purpose flour

2 green onions, white and green parts, thinly sliced

sea salt, to taste

INSTRUCTIONS

1. Place the bacon into a large skillet and cook over medium-low heat until it has rendered most of its fat, about 10 minutes. Transfer to a separate dish using a slotted spoon.

2. Increase the heat to medium-high and add the potatoes. Season generously with salt and pepper. Sear the potatoes until browned on all sides, about 10 minutes.

3. Add the vinegar and chicken stock to the pan and simmer for about 5 to 7 minutes, or until the potatoes are cooked through.

4. Remove 2 tablespoons of the cooking liquid and whisk it with the flour to form a slurry. Return this to the pan and cook until the sauce thickens and clings to the potatoes. Top with the green onions and bacon.

Field Corn Grits

A traditional breakfast dish in the American South, grits are made from corn. They take just 5 minutes to prepare and some time for baking, making them the perfect choice for getting your day going—or for pairing with hearty meat dishes like Beer-Grilled Chicken (page 92) or Pasture-Fed Lamb Kebabs (page 109) if you're feeling corny at night.

SERVES
6

PREP TIME
5 minutes

COOK TIME
45 to 60 minutes

3 quarts milk

1 quart heavy cream

1½ cups stone-ground polenta

1½ cups grits

pat of butter (optional)

1 cup roasted corn kernels, to garnish (optional)

sea salt, to taste

INSTRUCTIONS

1. Heat the milk and cream in a large, heavy-bottom pot until it comes to the barest simmer. Slowly pour in the polenta and grits, whisking constantly.

2. Cook for 45 to 50 minutes, or until the mixture is thick and the grains are very tender.

3. Season with salt. Serve topped with a pat of butter and roasted corn kernels, if using.

Harvest Dinner Rolls

SERVES
4 to 6

PREP TIME
25 minutes, plus
2 hours to rise

COOK TIME
20 minutes

An abundance of wheat is often due to a few lucky rolls. These dinner rolls include three different types of wheat for multidimensional flavor. They make for a great side dish for any feast when you just need some bread or for snacking, sandwiches, and more.

1½ cups all-purpose flour

½ cup whole wheat pastry flour

¼ cup buckwheat flour (optional), or increase whole-wheat flour

½ cup plus 2 tablespoons old-fashioned rolled oats

¼ cup dried potato flakes

1 teaspoon sea salt

2¼ teaspoons instant yeast or active dry yeast

2 tablespoons brown sugar

½ cup plus 2 tablespoons nonfat milk, warmed to 110°F

4 tablespoons melted butter, divided

1 large egg, whisked

INSTRUCTIONS

1. Combine the flours, oats, potato flakes, sea salt, yeast, and sugar in a large mixing bowl. Make a well in the center of the ingredients and add the milk, 2 tablespoons of the butter, and egg. Mix until thoroughly combined, then turn out onto a lightly floured surface and knead for 5 to 7 minutes, or until the dough is smooth and elastic.

2. Coat the interior of a clean bowl with oil and place the dough into it. Cover loosely with a towel and allow to rise for 60 minutes, or until it doubles in size.

3. Punch down the dough then divide it into 12 pieces, shaping each into a ball. Round into balls and place on a rimmed baking sheet lined with parchment paper or into a greased muffin tin. Cover with oiled plastic wrap and allow to rise for another 60 minutes.

4. Preheat the oven to 375°F. Brush the tops of the rolls with the remaining melted butter and bake for 20 minutes, until golden. Serve in a basket to pass around your feasting table.

Charred Summer Vegetables

Summer game nights mean using seasonal veggies that offer loads of flavor. In this case, they need just 15 minutes to prepare and less than that on the grill to thoroughly cook and slightly char them for that perfect summery flavor.

SERVES
4 to 6

PREP TIME
15 minutes

COOK TIME
6 to 8 minutes

1 medium eggplant, cut into 8 wedges

¼ cup plus 2 tablespoons extra-virgin olive oil, divided

¼ cup minced fresh basil

2 tablespoons good-quality balsamic vinegar

1 teaspoon minced fresh rosemary

1 clove garlic, minced

2 red bell peppers, cored and sliced

2 small zucchini, cut into 4 wedges each

1 small red onion, cut into ½-inch-thick rings

sea salt, to taste

freshly ground pepper, to taste

INSTRUCTIONS

1. Season the eggplant slices liberally with salt and set in a colander over the sink for at least 15 minutes or up to 1 hour.

2. Whisk ¼ cup of the olive oil with the basil, balsamic vinegar, rosemary, and garlic. Season with salt and pepper.

3. Preheat a gas or charcoal grill to medium-high heat.

4. Rinse the eggplant under cool water and wring each piece with your hands to remove excess moisture. Coat the eggplant, bell peppers, zucchini, and red onion in the remaining 2 tablespoons of olive oil. Grill them for 3 to 4 minutes on each side, or until deeply browned.

5. Toss the vegetables with the balsamic dressing and enjoy.

Crispy Cast-Iron Brussels Sprouts

In the world of CATAN, Ore is used to upgrade cities. In the home chef's kitchen, it's the go-to tool for making scrumptious recipes like this one. For some of that smoky grilled flavor without the hassle of the grill, you can make a batch of these delicious and crispy cast-iron Brussels sprouts. Technically, you could use any pan to make these, but the cast-iron is where that great charred/grilled flavor comes from and the crisp texture is perfected.

SERVES
4 to 6

PREP TIME
10 minutes

COOK TIME
20 to 25 minutes

3 tablespoons extra-virgin olive oil

1 pound brussels sprouts, trimmed and halved

1½ tablespoons good-quality balsamic vinegar

2 ounces Pecorino Romano, shaved

sea salt, to taste

freshly ground pepper, to taste

INSTRUCTIONS

1. Preheat the oven to 375°F.

2. Heat a cast-iron skillet over high heat for 2 to 3 minutes, or until it is very hot.

3. Add the oil to the pan. Add the brussels sprouts to the pan, cut side down. Season with salt and pepper.

4. Bake for 15 minutes.

5. Drizzle the sprouts with the balsamic vinegar, tossing to coat. Cook for another 3 to 5 minutes, or until the balsamic vinegar has caramelized but not burned. Top with the cheese and serve immediately.

PART IV

Hard-Won Desserts

Delectable Sweets and Baked Treats

Rocky Road Cookies

Chocolate-Covered Pretzel Logs

Homemade Fudge Bricks

Settlement Strudel

Cast-Iron Honey Cake

Orchard Apple Crisp

Pirate's Rum-Raisin Bread Pudding

LiBerry Galette

Customizable Hex Cookies

Fireside Banana Boats

Whole-Grain Carrot Cupcakes

Wild Blackberry Scones

Rocky Road Cookies

The longest road isn't always the smoothest, but persevering is worth the victory point reward! Break out these road-inspired cookies as you gather for a night of gameplay and merrymaking. They're like the famous ice cream, with gooey marshmallows and chocolate, plus nuts and that decadent cookie richness. To make them even more delicious, pair with vanilla ice cream, hot cocoa, or a glass of milk.

MAKES
2 dozen cookies

PREP TIME
10 minutes

COOK TIME
12 minutes

1 cup butter-flavored shortening

1 cup brown sugar

¾ cup white sugar

2 eggs

1 tablespoon vanilla extract

1¾ cups all-purpose flour

1 teaspoon sea salt

1 teaspoon baking soda

½ cup unsweetened cocoa powder

1 cup chocolate chips

¾ cup mini marshmallows, plus more for topping

½ cup roughly chopped almonds or pecans

INSTRUCTIONS

1. Preheat the oven to 350°F. Line a rimmed baking sheet with parchment paper.

2. Cream the shortening and sugars for 1 to 2 minutes using a hand or stand mixer.

3. Add the eggs and vanilla, and beat for another minute, until well mixed and fluffy.

4. Add the flour, sea salt, baking soda, and cocoa powder a little at a time until it is all integrated.

5. Stir in the chocolate chips, marshmallows, and almonds or pecans.

6. Shape the dough into 1- to 2-inch balls and place them on the baking sheet. Top with 2 or 3 mini marshmallows.

7. Bake for 12 minutes. Allow to cool on the pan for 5 minutes before transferring to a cooling rack.

Chocolate-Covered Pretzel Logs

For a super-easy, super-tasty treat, grab some pretzels, cream, and dark chocolate to make these salty and sweet pretzel "logs." They take just 10 minutes to make, from beginning to end, and anyone can help whip them up, even the youngest players.

SERVES
4 to 6

PREP TIME
5 minutes

COOK TIME
5 minutes

6 ounces dark chocolate, ideally 70 percent cacao, broken into pieces

¼ cup heavy cream

½ teaspoon vanilla extract

1 (16-ounce) bag pretzel logs (not the thin sticks)

V

INSTRUCTIONS

1. Heat the dark chocolate in a heavy-bottom saucepan over low heat until it just begins to melt.

2. Whisk in the heavy cream and stir until the chocolate is all melted and the cream is fully integrated. Add the vanilla extract and mix until fully combined.

3. Line a rimmed baking sheet with parchment paper.

4. Dip each of the pretzels into the chocolate, turning to coat, and then place on the baking sheet.

5. Allow to rest until the chocolate sets, about 10 minutes.

GLUTEN-FREE VARIATION: Use gluten-free pretzels to make them GF-friendly.

Homemade Fudge Bricks

Nothing says celebration like a pile of homemade fudge—whether it's holiday season, a game night, or just a special moment in life worth enjoying. And this quick, no-fail recipe is the perfect way to enjoy some chocolatey goodness without a lot of work or energy, and they are ready in pretty much the time it takes for them to cool off.

SERVES
4 to 6

PREP TIME
10 minutes,
plus 1½ hours to cool

COOK TIME
5 minutes

3 cups semisweet chocolate chips

1 (14-ounce) can sweetened condensed milk

2 teaspoons vanilla extract

½ cup finely chopped toasted pecans, divided (optional)

INSTRUCTIONS

1. Combine the chocolate chips, sweetened condensed milk, and vanilla in a medium saucepan over low heat. Stir until the chocolate is fully melted and mixed, about 5 minutes. Stir in the pecans, if using, saving 1 tablespoon for topping.

2. Pour the mixture into an 8 x 8-inch baking dish lined with plastic wrap or parchment paper. Top with the remaining pecans, if using. Refrigerate for at least 1½ hours or until set. Slice into squares.

Settlement Strudel

Just like you need a variety of resources to build a settlement, you'll need a variety of ingredients, including two kinds of raspberries, milk, cream cheese, and more, to make this flaky and tasty dessert come together. Using premade puff pastry, this decadent strudel is an easy recipe to draw crowds to the table. Whip some up in 10 minutes, bake, and serve as the meal's finished.

SERVES
4 to 6

PREP TIME
10 minutes

COOK TIME
25 minutes

1 sheet puff pastry

8 ounces cream cheese, softened

2 tablespoons milk

1 cup raspberry jam

2 cups raspberries

1 egg, whisked with 1 tablespoon of water

1 tablespoon granulated sugar

V

INSTRUCTIONS

1. Preheat the oven to 400°F. Line a baking sheet with parchment paper. Place the puff pastry on the baking sheet.

2. Whisk the cream cheese and milk so that it's of spreadable consistency.

3. Mentally divide the puff pastry into thirds. Spread the cream cheese down the center third of the puff pastry. Spread the raspberry jam over the cream cheese and then top with the raspberries.

4. Fold the outer thirds of the puff pastry over the center. Use a sharp knife to score the pastry.

5. Brush the pastry with the egg mixture, then sprinkle with sugar.

6. Bake for 25 minutes or until the top is golden brown.

143

Cast-Iron Honey Cake

Use your cast-iron skillet to create this delicious, easy honey cake in just 10 minutes plus cook time. The sweet dessert uses simple ingredients for a warm, buttery, cozy moment as you gather with others for a night of fun or when you just need some comfort food. For an extra zing of sweetness, top with a little Desert Jelly (page 64) or pair with your Smoked Game Legs (page 95) for a traditional country meal.

SERVES
4 to 6

PREP TIME
10 minutes

COOK TIME
30 to 35 minutes

½ cup plus 1 tablespoon butter, divided

2 cups plus 1 tablespoon all-purpose flour for dusting

1 cup honey

2 large eggs

¾ cup buttermilk

2 tablespoons vanilla extract

1 tablespoon baking powder

¾ teaspoon sea salt

INSTRUCTIONS

1. Preheat the oven to 325°F. Coat the inside of a 10- to 12-inch cast-iron skillet with 1 tablespoon of butter and dust with flour.

2. Beat the remaining butter, honey, eggs, buttermilk, and vanilla extract in a large bowl until thoroughly integrated. Sift in the flour, baking powder, and sea salt. Beat until no lumps remain. Pour the batter into the prepared pan. Bake for 30 to 35 minutes, or until a cake tester inserted in the center comes out clean.

Orchard Apple Crisp

What does a hard*core* day of gaming deserve? Dessert of course! This delicious after-dinner treat is worth all the *apple*-lause your family can offer, thanks to the sweet and tart zing of the Granny Smith apples paired with cinnamon and sugar. The rolled oats add some heartiness while the butter adds that soft texture that everyone will love. Serve it up with some fresh vanilla ice cream and some Late-Night Caramel Lattes (page 167) for the perfect evening.

SERVES
4 to 6

PREP TIME
20 minutes

COOK TIME
50 minutes

8 tablespoons butter, cold, divided

8 Granny Smith apples, peeled and cut into thin wedges

1 tablespoon ground cinnamon

8 tablespoons brown sugar, divided

¾ cup all-purpose flour

½ cup old-fashioned rolled oats

pinch of salt

INSTRUCTIONS

1. Preheat the oven to 350°F. Coat the interior of a cast-iron skillet with a tablespoon of butter. Spread the apples, cinnamon, and 2 tablespoons of brown sugar in the cast-iron skillet.

2. In a separate bowl, combine the remaining 6 tablespoons of brown sugar with the remaining butter, flour, oats, and salt. Mix until the mixture comes together and you can form it into clumps. Crumble the mixture over the apples. Bake for 50 minutes, or until the apples are tender and the top is golden brown.

Pirate's Rum-Raisin Bread Pudding

Time flies when you're having rum-raisin bread pudding! And it only takes 10 minutes to prepare, with less than an hour needed for cooking. Use premade French bread for best results and enjoy paired with your favorite sweet cocktail or Spiced Cider (page 172) for a cozy after-meal indulgence the whole party will delight in.

SERVES
4 to 6

PREP TIME
10 minutes

COOK TIME
40 minutes

2 tablespoons butter, divided

8 cups hand-torn French bread

2 cups milk

½ cup heavy cream

½ cup dark brown sugar

1 tablespoon vanilla extract

3 eggs

½ cup dark rum

1 cup raisins

vanilla ice cream, for serving

INSTRUCTIONS

1. Preheat the oven to 325°F. Coat the interior of a casserole dish with 1 tablespoon of butter.

2. Spread the French bread in the baking dish.

3. In a separate bowl, whisk the milk, cream, sugar, vanilla, eggs, and rum until thoroughly mixed. Sprinkle the raisins over the French bread (don't mix). Pour the milk mixture over the bread. Press down on it gently with a spatula to ensure all of the pieces are soaked with the milk and to gently disperse the raisins.

4. Cover tightly with aluminum foil and bake for 30 minutes. Uncover and brush the top of the dish with butter. Bake for another 10 minutes uncovered. Allow to cool for 15 minutes before serving with vanilla ice cream.

LiBerry Galette

Win the day and the crowd with this delicious French-style berry pastry and homage to the Library development card. It's an easy puff pastry offering, using your choice of berries, and takes just 10 minutes to make, plus 25 to 30 minutes to cook. Select well-known ones like blueberries, blackberries, or raspberries, and substitute your unique favorites like gooseberries, lingonberries, or boysenberries. Just make sure that if you use any tart berries, like cranberries, that you up the sugar a little bit.

SERVES
4 to 6

PREP TIME
10 minutes

COOK TIME
25 to 30 minutes

1 sheet puff pastry

4 cups raspberries, blackberries, and sliced strawberries

2 tablespoons granulated sugar

1 tablespoon cornstarch

zest of 1 lemon

whipped cream, for serving

powdered sugar, for serving

INSTRUCTIONS

1. Preheat the oven to 400°F.

2. Line a baking sheet with parchment paper and roll out the puff pastry.

3. In a medium mixing bowl, combine the berries, sugar, cornstarch, and lemon zest. Place the berries in the center of the puff pastry, leaving about 2 inches of dough around the perimeter.

4. Roll the edges of the puff pastry up over the edges of the fruit, pinching the corners to seal it.

5. Bake for 25 to 30 minutes or until the pastry is golden brown. Serve with whipped cream and sprinkle with powdered sugar.

Customizable Hex Cookies

Nothing is more iconic to CATAN than the resource hexes. These delicious sugar cookies with syrupy sweet glaze are the perfect way to enjoy some fun together as you customize your sweet treats. And they don't take as long as others to chill and prepare—just over an hour. Serve with a Late-Night Caramel Latte (page 167) or University-Friendly Hot Chocolate (page 171) for the perfect sweet pairing.

SERVES
4 to 6

PREP TIME
10 minutes, plus
30 minutes to chill

COOK TIME
30 minutes
(10 minutes for
each batch)

COOKIES

½ cup plus 2 tablespoons butter, chilled

½ cup plus 2 tablespoons white sugar

1 egg

1 teaspoon vanilla extract

2 cups all-purpose flour

½ teaspoon sea salt

½ teaspoon baking powder

glaze (see page 153)

COOKIES

1. Preheat the oven to 350°F. Line a rimmed baking sheet with parchment paper.

2. Cream the butter and sugar for 1 to 2 minutes using a hand or stand mixer.

3. Add the egg and vanilla, and beat for another minute, until well mixed and fluffy.

4. Add the flour, sea salt, and baking powder a little at a time until it is all integrated. Wrap the dough in plastic wrap and refrigerate for 30 minutes.

5. Roll the dough out on a parchment-paper lined work surface. Use a hex-shaped cookie cutter to cut out shapes. Carefully transfer to the baking sheet and bake for 10 minutes, or until gently browned at the edges. Allow to cool for 10 minutes before transferring to a cooling rack. Allow to cool completely before frosting with the glaze.

GLAZE

4 cups powdered sugar

3 tablespoons light corn syrup or honey

2 to 3 tablespoons milk or water

food coloring

GLAZE

1. Whisk the sugar, corn syrup, and milk in a medium mixing bowl.

2. Once it is thoroughly mixed and no lumps remain, add a few additional drops of milk or water until it reaches the desired consistency.

3. Divide the white glaze between smaller dishes and add food coloring to each to achieve desired colors according to the Food-Coloring Combinations below.

4. Use a squirt bottle to drizzle the glaze onto each cookie. Allow to cool thoroughly before storing.

FOOD-COLORING COMBINATIONS
BRICK RED: 10 parts red + 1 part black + 1 part yellow
FOREST GREEN: 10 parts green + 1 part black
AMBER GRAIN: 10 parts yellow + 1 part red
LAVENDER QUARTZ: 1 part red + 1 part blue

Fireside Banana Boats

SERVES
4

PREP TIME
10 minutes

COOK TIME
10 minutes

After a long day of building and trading, nothing is more a-peeling than relaxing by the fire with dessert! These banana boats take just 20 minutes to prepare and cook, making them even more desirable for a post-workday relaxation session. Combine your marshmallows, dark chocolate, and graham cracker squares and stuff those banana skins for a tasty, decadent, easy treat.

4 bananas

3 ounces dark chocolate, roughly chopped

½ cup mini marshmallows

4 graham cracker squares, crumbled

INSTRUCTIONS

1. Slice down one side of the banana peel just enough to open it. Repeat with the remaining bananas.

2. Stuff each one with a couple of tablespoons of chocolate and mini marshmallows.

3. Try to close the banana peels as best you can. Wrap each banana in tin foil and place over the campfire or grill and cook for 10 minutes.

4. Top each with crumbled graham crackers.

Whole-Grain Carrot Cupcakes

There's a reason why cupcakes are so popular and always have been: they're perfect for on-the-go snacking. These carrot cupcakes change the game up on your usual sweet treat using whole-grain wheat, dark brown sugar, and applesauce for a heavenly, dense delight, topped with gooey cream cheese frosting. Catanians of all ages will enjoy these vegetable-packed and field hex–inspired cakes at all hours.

MAKES
12 cupcakes

PREP TIME
15 minutes

COOK TIME
18 minutes

1⅓ cups whole wheat pastry flour

1 teaspoon baking soda

⅓ cup dark brown sugar

1 teaspoon ground cinnamon

¼ teaspoon freshly ground nutmeg

½ teaspoon sea salt

⅓ cup applesauce

2 eggs, whisked

½ cup canola oil

1 cup grated carrots

½ cup raisins (optional)

½ cup roughly chopped walnuts (optional)

½ cup butter, softened

1 (8-ounce) package cream cheese, softened

1 teaspoon vanilla extract

3 cups powdered sugar

½ cup caramel sauce

INSTRUCTIONS

1. Preheat the oven to 325°F. Line a 12-cup muffin tin with paper liners, ideally parchment paper.

2. Combine the flour, baking soda, sugar, cinnamon, nutmeg, and salt in a large mixing bowl. Make a well in the center of the ingredients and add the applesauce, eggs, and canola oil, stirring just until mixed.

3. Fold in the carrots, raisins, and walnuts. Divide the batter between muffin cups. Bake for 15 to 18 minutes, or until the cupcakes are golden brown and a cake tester comes out nearly clean.

4. To make the frosting, combine the butter, cream cheese, and vanilla in the bowl of a stand mixer and mix until thoroughly combined. Sift in the powdered sugar and continue mixing until all of it is integrated. Swirl the caramel sauce into the frosting. Wait until the cupcakes are completely cooled before frosting.

DID YOU KNOW? In 2022, the CATAN World Championship was held on the island of Malta. The winner was Hamish Dean of New Zealand.

V

Wild Blackberry Scones

Foraging for your own wild blackberries may be a bit challenging, but you're likely to find some amazing berries at your local farmer's market or specialty store. And when you whip them into these scones, you'll be grateful for that wild fruit flavor. Serve them up as a dessert or pair them with Explorer's Lemonade (page 164), Hot Mulled Wine (page 176), or Knight-Cap Hot Toddy (page 184) for a sweet end to the gathering.

SERVES
4 to 6

PREP TIME
15 minutes

COOK TIME
20 minutes

2 cups all-purpose flour

½ cup granulated sugar

¾ teaspoon sea salt

1 tablespoon baking powder

½ cup butter, chilled, cut into 8 pieces

½ cup heavy cream

1 egg, whisked

1½ teaspoons vanilla extract

1 tablespoon minced fresh rosemary (optional)

1 cup blackberries

whipped cream, for serving

V

INSTRUCTIONS

1. Preheat the oven to 400°F. Line a baking sheet with parchment paper.

2. Combine the flour, sugar, salt, and baking powder in a food processor. Pulse once or twice to combine. Add the butter and pulse a few times until the mixture resembles coarse sand. Turn it out into a bowl, making a well in the center of the ingredients. Stir in the cream, egg, and vanilla extract, mixing until combined. Fold in the rosemary, if using, and the blackberries.

3. Cover a clean work surface with a large sheet of parchment paper. Transfer the dough to the parchment paper. Gently roll it out to about 1½ inches thick. Cut the dough into wedges. Carefully transfer the parchment to a baking sheet (a rimless sheet works best here to easily slide it off the counter). Separate the scones with ample space between each one.

4. Bake for 20 minutes, or until golden brown. Allow to cool for at least 20 minutes before serving with whipped cream.

PART V

Cheers for Victory

Boozy Cocktails and Refreshing Nonalcoholic Beverages

Explorer's Lemonade

Late-Night Caramel Latte

Ocean Water

University-Friendly Hot Chocolate

Spiced Cider

Victory Point Punch

Hot Mulled Wine

Port Wine Spritz

Cherrywood-Smoked Old-Fashioned

Desert Margarita

Knight-Cap Hot Toddy

Robber Roy

Explorer's Lemonade

After a long day of working on the roads, in an office, or in the garden, a sweet, tangy, cold lemonade will really hit the spot. It's the perfect refreshing drink, made from scratch, for the best balance of sweet and tart. It pairs perfectly with the Seafarer's Summer Salad (page 82) or as a stand-alone treat.

(page 82)

SERVES
4 to 6

PREP TIME
10 minutes, plus 30 minutes to steep

COOK TIME
5 minutes

2 cups granulated sugar

6 cups water, divided

peel of 1 lemon (yellow part only, not the white pith)

2 cups freshly squeezed lemon juice

INSTRUCTIONS

1. Heat the sugar, 2 cups of water, and lemon peel in a small saucepan over medium heat until the sugar is dissolved. Set aside to steep for 30 minutes, or chill overnight.

2. Remove the peel from the simple syrup. Pour it into a pitcher with the lemon juice and 4 additional cups of cold water. Serve over ice.

Late-Night Caramel Latte

When you need a sweet pick-me-up to keep the energy flowing and the game night going, whip up a mug (or batch) of Late-Night Caramel Lattes. They use decadently sweet caramel syrup for flavor and a punch of espresso to get the caffeine boost you're craving. Each one takes just 7 minutes to make, with no fancy equipment required. Pour out one with your Rocky Road Cookies (page 136) or Settlement Strudel (page 143) for an extra rush of energy.

SERVES
1

PREP TIME
5 minutes

COOK TIME
2 minutes

1 cup 2 percent or whole milk

2 tablespoons caramel syrup

2 ounces espresso or ½ cup coffee

whipped cream, for serving

INSTRUCTIONS

1. Heat the milk and caramel in a small saucepan over medium heat until it is steaming.

2. Remove from the heat before it comes to a simmer.

3. Stir in the espresso or coffee.

4. Pour into a serving mug and top with whipped cream.

Ocean Water

Sometimes the road to victory is via the sea. Celebrate a settlement on a harbor with another sip of this bright-blue ocean-themed punch. Each sip will transport you to sandy beaches, bubbling waves, tropical vibes, and the oh-so-sweet taste of fruit grown on palm trees. This ocean water is safe to drink (and kid friendly)!

SERVES
4

PREP TIME
5 minutes

1 cup pineapple juice, strained from canned pineapple chunks, chilled

2 cups blue Hawaiian Punch, chilled

2 cups club soda, chilled

8 to 12 pineapple chunks

4 cocktail umbrellas

INSTRUCTIONS

1. Mix the pineapple juice, Hawaiian Punch, and club soda in a pitcher.

2. Divide between serving cups.

3. Thread 2 to 3 pineapple chunks onto the ends of the cocktail umbrellas and place into each drink.

University-Friendly Hot Chocolate

SERVES
4

PREP TIME
5 minutes

COOK TIME
2 to 3 minutes

Catch up on your studies with this delicious, alcohol-free drink. This cozy and sugary hot chocolate is perfect for any cold, wintery night—whether you're cramming for exams or procrastinating with your friends. Drink up with the sweet, dark chocolate taking the stage while the peppermint adds notes of the season.

4 cups whole milk

¼ cup cocoa powder (not cocoa mix)

¼ cup granulated sugar

5 ounces dark chocolate, preferably 70 percent cacao, roughly chopped, or 5 ounces semi-sweet chocolate chips

1 teaspoon peppermint extract

whipped cream, for serving

4 peppermint sticks, for serving

INSTRUCTIONS

1. Combine all of the ingredients except for the whipped cream and peppermint sticks in a medium saucepan over medium-low heat and bring almost to a simmer, whisking constantly until the chocolate is melted, about 2 to 3 minutes.

2. Divide between serving mugs and top with whipped cream and a peppermint stick.

Spiced Cider

SERVES
8

PREP TIME
5 minutes

COOK TIME
4 hours, or
30 minutes

This autumnal beverage is best served on cool, crisp nights. The warm wash of the fire, the cool tinge in the air—nothing celebrates the season better than a zingy drink like this. Pair with your favorite sweet treat, like Cast-Iron Honey Cake (page 144), or let it provide that sweet finish for a poultry dish. See step two for instructions on how to make this drink family friendly!

2 quarts apple cider

4 cinnamon sticks

1-inch piece of ginger, sliced into thin coins

1 orange, with peel, sliced

1 teaspoon whole cloves

1 cup bourbon or dark rum (optional)

INSTRUCTIONS

1. Place the cider, cinnamon, ginger, orange, and cloves into a slow cooker and cook on low for 4 hours. Or place it into a heavy pot on the stove and simmer for 30 minutes over medium-low heat.

2. Stir in the bourbon or rum, if using, and serve. If serving to adults, allow each guest to add 1 ounce of bourbon to each 8-ounce mug of cider.

Victory Point Punch

This big-batch cocktail will make everyone feel like a winner! Combining cranberry juice, orange juice, pomegranate juice, fresh fruit, and white rum or vodka, this sweet and tangy drink will keep the merriment going. Skip the liquor for an alcohol-free variation that's just as tasty and much more appropriate for the littlest explorers!

SERVES
8

PREP TIME
10 minutes

4 ounces orange juice concentrate

2 cups sweetened cranberry juice

1 cup pomegranate juice

1 cup vodka or white rum (optional)

4 cups club soda

1 orange, sliced

1 cup cranberries

1 large sprig fresh rosemary

INSTRUCTIONS

1. Combine the orange juice concentrate, cranberry juice, pomegranate juice, and vodka or rum, if using, in a large pitcher or punch bowl, stirring until well mixed.

2. Add the club soda, orange, cranberries, and rosemary. Serve over ice.

Hot Mulled Wine

Buy a development card or save up for a city? You never know how long it might take to gather the resources. While you mull it over, grab a mug of this tasty spiced mulled wine. Perfect for a cool autumn night or holiday afternoon, this rich and spicy beverage is an old-world classic that evokes all the good feels of happy days past, tossing in an apple for good measure. Make it the spotlight or serve alongside your favorite holiday treats like Pirate's Rum-Raisin Bread Pudding (page 148) or Orchard Apple Crisp (page 147).

SERVES
4 to 6

PREP TIME
10 minutes, plus
30 minutes to sit

COOK TIME
30 minutes

½ cup granulated sugar

2 whole cinnamon sticks

1 apple, cored and sliced

1 teaspoon whole cloves

1 orange, with peel, sliced

1 bottle red wine

INSTRUCTIONS

1. Place all of the ingredients into the slow cooker, stir to mix, and cook on low for 30 minutes.

2. Stir to mix, place the mulled wine into a heavy pot on the stove, allow the ingredients to sit for 30 minutes, then bring to a simmer. Immediately remove from the heat so as not to cook off the alcohol.

Port Wine Spritz

Invest in some quality port; you've already invested in some harbors in CATAN, and you'll be delighted by this sparkling spritzer. It uses fresh fruit, full-bodied, sweet port, and club soda to sparkle and delight. Make it ahead so it has plenty of time to chill, and enjoy alongside Cast-Iron Honey Cake (page 144) or Customizable Hex Cookies (page 152) for a delightfully sweet duo.

SERVES
1

PREP TIME
5 minutes, plus
45 minutes
to chill

4 to 5 cherries, strawberries, or apple slices

3 ounces port

1 cup club soda

INSTRUCTIONS

1. Place the fruit and port into a nonreactive dish and set aside for 45 minutes to overnight in the refrigerator to infuse the port with the fruit flavors.

2. Transfer the fruit and port to a glass and top with the club soda and a handful of ice.

DID YOU KNOW? Inhabitants of Catan as well as CATAN fans are named Catanians.

Cherrywood-Smoked Old-Fashioned

SERVES
1

PREP TIME
10 minutes, plus
1 hour to smoke and
overnight to chill

This stiff drink evokes smoky memories of days long past. Using wood chips to actually smoke the old-fashioned might tell you why. The drink takes just 10 minutes to prepare but you'll smoke it for an hour and let chill overnight for the perfect cherry-whiskey drink. Cherrywood is the top choice here, but alderwood is a common woodchip for smoking. Hickory or oak will work as well.

2 cups wood chips

1 pound fresh cherries, unpitted

1 cup sugar

1 cup water

2 ounces whiskey or bourbon

2 dashes Angostura bitters

INSTRUCTIONS

1. Prepare the wood chips in a smoker box on a grill. Place the cherries onto a vegetable rack or aluminum tray and smoke for 1 hour.

2. In a medium saucepan, heat the sugar and water, and stir until the sugar dissolves. Add the smoked cherries, cover, and chill overnight.

3. To make the cocktail, place a few cherries into the bottom of a glass. Top with 2 to 3 teaspoons of the smoked cherry simple syrup, the whiskey, and the bitters. Stir gently to mix and top with a handful of ice cubes.

NOTE: For the steps to make a smoker with a gas or charcoal grill, see page 95.

Desert Margarita

The Desert hex doesn't produce anything that will help you win a round of CATAN, but you can produce this prickly pear cactus-infused margarita in its honor. The intricate flavors of fresh lime juice, coarse salt, tequila, triple sec, and that unique prickly pear syrup make this an unforgettable drink for the whole group.

1 ounce freshly squeezed (not bottled) lime juice, plus more for the rim of the glass

Tajín seasoning, chile seasoning, or coarse salt, to rim the glass

2 ounces good-quality tequila

1 ounce cointreau or triple sec

½ ounce prickly pear syrup

INSTRUCTIONS

1. Wet the rim of the glass with lime juice and dip it in the coarse salt or seasoning.

2. In a shaker, combine the lime juice, tequila, cointreau or triple sec, and prickly pear syrup with ice. Shake until well chilled.

3. Place additional ice into the glass and pour the shaken cocktail mixture into it. Serve immediately.

Knight-Cap Hot Toddy

Whether or not the Largest Army card is part of your game-winning strategy, this comforting Knight-cap cocktail will have you in a good mood—win or lose. This drink is the perfect finish to the evening, using dark rum or whiskey, honey, and fresh lemon to send you off to dreamland. Sip quietly by the fire or pair with Whole-Grain Carrot Cupcakes (page 158) for a late-night snack before drifting off to sleep.

> SERVES
> 1
>
> PREP TIME
> 5 minutes
>
> COOK TIME
> 2 minutes

1 cup water

1½ ounces dark rum or whiskey

1 tablespoon honey

2 to 3 teaspoons lemon juice, to taste

slice of 1 lemon

INSTRUCTIONS

1. Bring the water to a simmer (some will evaporate).

2. Pour it into a heatproof mug and stir in the rum or whisky, honey, and lemon juice.

3. Top with the lemon wedge.

DID YOU KNOW? There are four main expansions available in addition to the core CATAN base game and many scenarios that add even more stories and adventures.

Robber Roy

The truth is that the Robber is a harmless fellow who is merely taken advantage of by Catanians for the sake of their own benefit. He is pushed around from terrain to terrain, unable to escape his sometimes quite-harsh destiny. Craft up this take on the classic Rob Roy cocktail and make a toast to CATAN's robber—the game would be a lot less fun without him, after all! It just takes 5 minutes and 4 simple ingredients to make. Serve solo or pair with Homemade Fudge Bricks (page 140) for the perfect sweet and strong combo.

SERVES
1

PREP TIME
5 minutes

2 ounces blended Scotch whisky

1 ounce sweet vermouth

2 dashes Angostura bitters

lemon twist

INSTRUCTIONS

1. Place the whisky, vermouth, and bitters into a shaker with ice.

2. Shake until the liquors are well chilled.

3. Pour into a martini or rocks glass and garnish with a lemon twist.

Recipe Index

CATAN